UNDERSTANDING THE TURKISH-ARMENIAN CONTROVERSY OVER 1915

Mustafa Serdar PALABIYIK

Beta

This edition published 2015

ISBN: 978 - 605 - 333 - 208 - 4

Mustafa Serdar Palabıyık

Understanding The Turkish-Armenian Controversy Over 1915

Cover Photographs Front : The Ancient City of Ani, Seyhan Ahen

Printing and Binding
Ertem Basım Yayın Dağıtım San. Tic. Ltd. Şti.
Eskişehir Yolu 40. Km. Başkent Organize Sanayi Bölgesi
22. Cadde No: 6, Malıköy / Sincan / Ankara
(Certificate Number: 26886) (0312) 640 16 23

Beta Basım Yayım Dağıtım A.Ş. (Certificate Number: 16136)
Narlıbahçe Sokak Damga Binası No: 11
Cağaloğlu - İSTANBUL
Tel : (0-212) 511 54 32 - 519 01 77
Fax: (0-212) 511 36 50
www.betayayincilik.com

Mustafa Serdar Palabıyık

Palabıyık graduated from the Middle East Technical University, Department of International Relations and he completed his MSc and PhD degrees in the same department. His research interests include Turkish-Armenian relations, Ottoman diplomatic history and Turkish foreign policy. He is the author of various articles on Turkish-Armenian relations, published in *Review of Armenian Studies* and *Ermeni Araştırmaları*, as well as on Ottoman diplomatic history, published in *New Perspectives on Turkey, Bilig* and *Middle Eastern Studies*. He is currently working as an assistant professor in TOBB Economics and Technology University, Department of International Relations.

Abbreviations

ASALA	The Armenian Secret Army for the Liberation of Armenia
BOA	Başbakanlık Osmanlı Arşivi-Prime Ministry Ottoman Archives
DH ŞFR	Dahiliye Nezareti, Şifreli Yazışma – Ministry Of Internal Affairs, Codec Telegram
EUM ŞFR	Emniyet Umumiye Müdürlüğü, Şifreli Yazışma – The General Directorate of Security, Coded Telegram
CC	Constitutional Council of France
CFI	Court of First Instance of the Court of Justice of the European Union
CUP	Committee of Union and Progress
ECHR	European Court of Human Rights
FO	Foreign Office
ICTY	International Criminal Tribunal for the former Yugoslavia
JCAG	Justice Commandos of the Armenian Genocide
MMZC	Meclis-i Mebusan Zabıt Ceridesi – Proceedings of the Chamber of Deputies
NATO	North Atlantic Treaty Organization
PFA	Policy Forum Armenia
USSR	The Union of Soviet Socialist Republics
USA	United States of America

Contents

Foreword

This short but valuable study deals with several critical aspects of the "Armenian question" as it has developed from the late 19th century. Most of them have no place in the "western" cultural mainstream, where ignorance and bias battle with each other for preeminence. In the short term this works very much to the advantage of the propagandist and the soi-disant "historian" who can omit, distort, suppress and twist without any fear of being challenged. The 19th century narrative on this issue was built on a foundation of untruth bordering on hysteria, the only word appropriate to describe the anti-Turkish and anti-Islamic prejudice that swept Britain during the 1890s. The dominant 20th century mainstream narrative was built on these shaky foundations. The narrative is linear, with victims on one side and perpetrators on the other: the trail leads directly to truth with a capital T. Everyone seems to know what the truth is except one of the principal actors in this drama, the Turks. Their disagreement with the mainstream narrative is put down to a stubborn refusal to come to terms with the truth as defined by western governments, parliaments and media, there being no other truths in the telling of this tragic story.

The "genocide scholars" are a particular story. One can plough through their books without finding scarcely a mention of events in which Muslims were the victims of what these days would be called "ethnic cleansing" or even genocide. No other phrases would be suitable to describe the massacres and depopulation of the Ottoman provinces of southeastern Europe in 1877-78 and again during the Balkan Wars of 1912-13. Neither is there any engagement with what Arnold Toynbee called a "war of extermination" of the Turks and an Inter-Allied Committee of Inquiry described as the "systematic plan of destruction of the Turkish villages and extinction of the Moslem population" following the Greek invasion of Anatolia in 1919.[1]

In the middle of this bloody period of history stands the "Armenian question", never just about the Armenians anyway because it involved the fate of Turks and Kurds and Muslims of other ethnic descriptions who killed Armenians but also died at their hands. The causes of death of Christians and Muslims were the same: massacre, disease, malnutrition and combat during the second-level intra-ethnic war being fought by the civilian population. The tawdry debate over the numbers of dead continues: was it 1.5 million Armenians - a completely unrealistic figure seeing that this would mean virtually the entire Ottoman Armenian population died between 1914-18 when in fact hundreds of thousands survived the war - or was it 800,000 or 600,000 or was it perhaps even less? How many Ottoman Muslim civilians might have died during the same period of history does not figure at all in the mainstream narrative but about 2.5 million would be

---

1   Quoted in my book *The Unmaking of the Middle East. A History of Western Disorder in Arab Lands* (Berkeley: University of California Press, 2008), pp. 75-76.

a starting point for debate. Ottoman documents indicate that hundreds of thousands were massacred. The evidence here is far more solid than the lurid accusations born of hearsay that characterized the Bryce propaganda report of 1916, whose foundation was the authority of a respected historian and former ambassador who was still willing to lie and deceive for his country.

One should not doubt the hard core of truth lying beneath the embellishments, exaggerations and lies in the Armenian account of history but neither should one doubt the hard core of truth in the evidence of Muslim suffering at the hands of Armenians. Were the readers of books on this issue allowed to know that Armenians were the perpetrators of large-scale violence as well as its victims, their understanding of what was going on would have to be affected. It is not just the Balkan governments of 1912-13 or the Greek government of 1919-22 who could be accused of setting in motion genocidal wars. The savagery of Armenian attacks on Muslims during the Russian-Armenian occupation of northeastern Anatolia shocked their Russian sponsors. The motive of revenge – "give to them [the Kurds] what they have given us" as Armenian women told their insurgent menfolk – set up a reciprocal motive of revenge amongst the Kurds and other Muslims. A high Russian official spoke of the Armenian "predilection" for massacring and looting: it seemed to him that Armenian nationalists wanted "to exterminate all the Muslim residents of the areas we occupied", with their savagery only provoking "desperate Kurdish resistance" that complicated Russian military operations.[2]

Ottoman forces able to return to the east in 1918 entered ruined cities strewn with corpses. Yet despite this background of general and widespread inter-ethnic brutality between 1914-1922, despite the prima facie evidence of an intention to destroy Muslims - mostly Kurds and Turks - by the Balkan states in 1912-13, by the Armenians during the war, by the Greeks after 1919 and by even certain Christian groups caught up in the machinations of the entente powers, it is only "the Turks" who stand accused of genocide.

The "genocide" has over the years become the cornerstone of Armenian nationalism. As Dr. Palabıyık points out, it is the central binding element of Armenian diaspora communities, simultaneously locking Armenian governments into a position of inflexibility regarding relations with Turkey in particular. Armenia is a poor landlocked country that needs to develop strong trade and diplomatic relations with Turkey but cannot because of the blockage created by the insertion of the "g-word" into every transaction that takes place. The benefits of normalization with Turkey are clear and it should surely be possible for parallel tracks to develop: one focusing on contemporary realities and needs and the other the continuing argument over what happened in 1914-18.

---

2   Michael A. Reynolds, *Shattering Empires. The Clash and Collapse of the Ottoman and Russian Empires 1908-1918* (New York: Cambridge University Press, 2011), pp. 156-158.

Instead, the two are conflated, frustrating efforts on both sides to create a healthier relationship but doing more practical damage to the weaker material country than to Turkey. The Armenian Republic should surely be able to defend its view of history without sacrificing relations with a country that did not exist in 1915 and is populated by a people who in no way can be held responsible for what happened during the First World War. Turkish intellectuals and journalists have issued their own statement of regret and remorse for the crimes committed by their forefathers and only this year, Turkey's Prime Minister, Recep Tayyip Erdogan, offered his condolences to the descendants of Ottoman Armenians. No reciprocal healing statements have yet come from the Armenian side, which indeed does not even acknowledge the scale of Ottoman Muslim suffering at Armenian hands.

A central issue is what to call the massacres. The Armenian expression "Meds Yeghern" literally translates as "great calamity" but in usage is taken by the Armenians to mean genocide, defined in Article Two of the UN Convention on the Prevention and Punishment of the Crime of Genocide (1948) as acts committed with intent to destroy "in whole or part a national, ethnical, racial or religious group."

The phrase "intent to destroy" is the key. Dr. Palabıyık goes into this issue in some detail. He reaches back into history to show that within the Ottoman millet system, Christians and Jews enjoyed broad freedoms as long as they respected the sovereign rights of the sultan. The main lines of demarcation were socio-economic rather than religious: within the palace circle, Armenian bankers and bureaucrats had far more in common with the Muslims pashas than they did with their own impoverished co-religionists. They abhorred the revolutionary committees when they appeared on the scene in the late 19th and consequently were regarded by them as "traitors." If Armenian villagers suffered at the hands of negligent or corrupt administrators and Kurdish tribal chieftains in the eastern provinces so did the Muslims but in the age of Christian evangelism in the 19th century it was only the suffering of the first that interested missionaries and the "humanitarians" in Europe and the United States. At the same time religious faith was potentially incendiary, and when the embers were stirred, as they were by the Armenian revolutionary committees in the 1880s and 1890s, it was small Armenian communities living amongst the Muslim majority who were most at risk when the embers burst into flames.

In all of Ottoman history there is no parallel with the racial antagonism generated against Jews in German lands since at least the time of Martin Luther. Far from being the victims of exclusion, discrimination and persecution, the Armenians were regarded by the sultans and their governments as the "faithful millet", with members of the community in Istanbul rising to high positions in the bureaucracy and enjoying privileged access to the palace circle. After 1839 Ottoman governments sought to create a citizenry that had equal rights before the law irrespective of ethnic or religious background. This was not an aberration but a process that continued through the constitutional revolution of 1908, with Armenians and other Christians resisting the loss of privileges threatened by the abolition of the Capitulations despite their avowed support for the equality of all citizens before the law. With war approaching, the Ottoman government tried hard to persuade the Armenian revolutionary committees to remain loyal to the Ottoman war effort. Even when it was clear that they had decided to throw their lot in with Russia, they were allowed to operate freely until the Van uprising in the spring of 1915.

Van was a turning point. The dithering over what to do about the Armenian insurgency had to stop. Van had been lost to the Russians and other cities might follow. One of the most important sections of this book deals with the "relocation" from the viewpoint of military necessity. Was the removal from their homes of so many people justified by the disruption of the war effort from behind the lines? Edward Erickson has taken up this question in his recent book, *Ottomans and Armenians. A Study in Counterinsurgency* (New York: Palgrave Macmillan, 2013) and believes that it was. Fighting a war to the death on several fronts, the Ottoman military command could no longer tolerate sabotage from behind the lines. Shortly after the fall of Van, on the recommendation of the military, the government issued the "relocation" order. Disruption, dislocation and massacres of Armenians as they were moved south towards Syria followed. Was this what the Ottoman government had in mind when it issued this order? What was its intention – to destroy the

Armenians or to move them away from the front line and deprive the insurgents of their support base?

The Nazis spelt out their genocidal intentions at the Wannsee conference of 1942. Propagandists have tried to show that the ruling Committee of Union and Progress government took a similar decision at a meeting held in Istanbul in early 1915. Their accusations, built on forged documents and their own suppositions and speculation, do not withstand even cursory scrutiny. Neither can it be assumed from the calamitous consequences of the "relocation" that the government in Istanbul knew what these consequences would be. Amongst those who do not go as far as insisting that the Ottoman government actually took a decision to wipe out the Armenians the argument is strong that they "must have known". What they "must have known" remains obscure. They "must have known" how difficult it would be to move such a large number of people in war time but there are many things they could not have known in advance or for which they were not prepared. That they *should* have known is a separate question: even if it did not realize in advance what the consequences of its decision to "relocate" the Armenians would be, the wartime Ottoman government still has to be held responsible. This is simply the nature of government.

All the evidence points in the direction of a decision being taken after the Van uprising to remove the Armenians but not to destroy them. That "intent to destroy" was not the motive of the wartime government is bolstered by documents in the Ottoman archives. Provincial officials are sent lengthy instructions on the need to care for the Armenians during their journey south. When reports came in of attacks on the convoys they are told to give the Armenians greater protection. Finally the government set up three commissions of inquiry which resulted in more than 1600 people being court-martialled for the crimes they had allegedly committed: hundreds of people were jailed and more than 60 were sentenced to death. It is simply not credible that a government allegedly committed to the annihilation of the Armenians would simultaneously punish its own soldiers and civil servants for mistreating them. As Dr. Palabıyık points out, quoting international law specialist John Quigley, "without the "intent to destroy", no crime can be considered as genocide."

It remains extraordinary that some parliaments around the world whose members can only fairly be described as knowing nothing of Ottoman history, next to nothing of the Ottoman experience of the First World War and very little of international law, should somehow regard themselves as competent to pass judgment on the fate of the Armenians. It is just as extraordinary that they seem to have no idea or no concern for the fate of the millions of Muslim victims of this war. There is nothing new about this. In the 19th century "humanitarians" had little or nothing to say about the assaults on the Muslim population of southeastern Europe. William Gladstone's outrage at the "Bulgarian atrocities" of 1876 was not followed by outrage at the far greater crimes committed against Muslims by the Russian army and the brigands following in their wake.

Ottoman Christians rarely benefited from outside intervention in their name. In the late 19th century distant support encouraged the Armenians to take up positions that were untenable and dangerous for a small minority. Britain had led the interventionist charge on behalf of the Armenians since the 1870s but by the time communal relations collapsed in the 1890s its strategic priorities had changed. It never was going to intervene on behalf of the Armenians just for their sake and when the crisis broke in the 1890s it simply walked away.

During the First World War the Russian and British governments showed no concern for the vulnerable position Armenians were putting themselves in as a minority rising up against the majority. The Assyrians as a much smaller community were even more vulnerable but got nothing back for their contribution to the Entente war effort. They ended up abandoned in Iraq. France had its eyes on the cotton fields and deep water ports of the eastern Mediterranean and in late November 1918 invaded what is now southeastern Turkey in the name of returning the Armenians to their Cilician homeland and bringing them under French protection. This venture broke against the wall of Turkish national resistance, but while the French soldiers could go back to their own country, the Armenians they had ostensibly taken under their wing were again scattered and dispersed to the four winds. There are surely lessons to be learnt here for Middle Eastern minorities tempted to succumb to the blandishments of distant governments.

Parliamentary support for "genocide" resolutions that have come straight out of the propagandist's information kit has only aggravated relations between Armenians and Turks and their respective governments. Are the politicians who involve themselves in this issue really thinking of the best interests of Armenians and Turks? Can even Armenians believe this? Dr. Palabıyık's study is an opportunity for readers to look afresh at the central issues in what perseveres as a volatile issue in international relations.

Jeremy Salt, May, 2014

Jeremy Salt is a visiting Associate Professor in Middle Eastern History and Politics at Bilkent University. He is the author of *Imperialism, Evangelism and the Ottoman Armenians 1878-1896* (1993) and *The Unmaking of the Middle East: A History of Western Disorder in Arab Lands* (2009). His articles appeared in *Middle East Policy, Third World Quarterly, Middle Eastern Studies, Current History, Journal of Arabic, Islamic and Middle Eastern Studies, Arena* and *Palestine Chronicle*.

Understanding the Turkish-Armenian Controversy Over 1915

Introduction

Every nation has had both glorious and sorrowful days in its history. Glory and sorrow contribute to the memory of nations and create a common basis for pride and grief. These emotions strengthen the sense of being a nation. Both Turks and the Armenians have such memories from their pasts. However, these memories, shaped by a common history that had been experienced predominantly in peace for more than eight centuries, are shadowed by a common grief which has come out because of the severe experiences befell on these two nations during the First World War.

The relocation of the Ottoman Armenians in 1915 is one of the most significant and controversial issues in Turkish-Armenian relations. Hundreds of thousands of Armenians were relocated under extremely harsh conditions. Their casualties were high either because of ill-treatment, epidemics, and malnutrition or else because of attacks by bandits and inter-communal clashes between Turks, Kurds and Armenians. Meanwhile, hundreds of thousands of Muslims living in Eastern Anatolia endured similar grief. They were killed by Armenian guerillas, Armenian volunteers and regular Armenian soldiers of the Russian army or they died as a result of disease, hunger, and other debilitating wartime conditions. While the Ottoman-Turkish historical narrative of these years does draw attention to the suffering of these two nations and focuses on the mutuality of their grievances, the Armenian narrative insists on the recognition of the 1915 relocation and treatment of the Armenian community by the Ottoman Empire during World War I as genocide. While the Ottoman-Turkish narrative acknowledges the suffering of the Ottoman Armenians, the Armenian narrative totally disregards the sufferings to which Muslims were exposed at exactly the same time.

Isolating the painful memories of the Ottoman Armenians during World War I from its historical context would be misleading. Under war time conditions, the Armenians were not the only group experiencing conditions of extreme severity. The World War I resulted in the arduous process of the dissolution of several multiethnic Empires, including the Austro-Hungarian, Russian and the Ottoman Empires. Not only minor ethnic groups (in the Ottoman case, Armenians, Greeks, etc.), but also the dominant group (in the Ottoman case, the Muslim Turks) suffered significantly during this process of disintegration. The second decade of the twentieth century was an age of great disasters for the regions once ruled by the Ottoman Empire. Hundreds of thousands of Turks and Muslims were forcibly expelled from the Balkans and experienced serious losses in 1912-1913. This process was remembered as the *Büyük Felaket* (the Great Disaster). This was followed by the mass relocation of the Armenians resulting in the loss of hundreds of thousands of lives and similarly being given the name in Armenian of *Meds Yeghern* (the Great Calamity). Finally, the ultimate defeat of the Greek armies in Anatolia resulted in a massive exodus of the Greek population of Western Anatolia, even before the compulsory exchange of populations, known to the Greeks as the *Mikroasiatiki Katastrofi* (the Asia Minor Catastrophe). In other words, whether they were small or large, different nations and ethnic groups of the region had bitter experiences in the decade between 1912 and 1922. Armenian suffering must be examined within this context.

Moreover, recognizing the Armenian relocation as genocide and then also presenting this claim as an exclusive historical truth are equally debatable. First and foremost, "genocide" is a legal concept. Its definition, content and legal methods for its punishment have been clearly stipulated in the 1948 UN Convention on the Prevention and the Punishment of the Crime of Genocide (from here on, the Genocide Convention). Considering the literature that exists on the crime of genocide, one may conclude that identifying a particular event as genocide is extremely difficult, unless certain and undisputable evidence exists to place the event clearly within the legal definition of genocide.

Hence, the Armenian relocation can be debated within various perspectives: historically, politically, or socio-economically. Its rationale, its method, its discursive and practical foundations may be discussed among historians. However, when it comes to labeling the relocation as genocide, legal analysis is required. Moreover, according to the Genocide Convention, genocide is a crime and should be punished only by competent domestic or international courts. Since there has never been a court decision with regard to the 1915 relocation

"Genocide" is a legal concept. Its definition, content and legal methods for its punishment have been clearly stipulated in the 1948 UN Convention.

which recognized it as genocide, this concept cannot be used to denote these events in a way which gives rise to a legal result.

This study tries to answer the question whether the 1915 relocation fits into the genocide definition of the Genocide Convention. While doing so, it intends to remain within the confines of the Convention and compares Turkish and Armenian narratives on this legal basis. It is designed as a manual, which briefly summarizes the debates with regard to the 1915 relocation. This study consists of seven chapters. The first chapter is a legal introduction to the concept of genocide, in which two basic components of this specific crime, namely the "motive to destroy" and the "intent to destroy", are briefly defined. The second chapter examines in detail the issue of the "motive to destroy" and tries to answer whether racially-prejudiced anti-Armenian discourse existed in the Ottoman Empire, something which could have led to an attempt at the extermination of the Ottoman Armenian community. This is followed by a third chapter closely analyzing the "intent to destroy", which not only questions the open declaration of intent but also the circumstantial evidence for labeling such an act as genocidal. Through a closer look at pre-World War I Anatolia and the policies of the Ottoman administration towards the Armenians in this period, "the intent to destroy" argument will be assessed. The fourth chapter focuses on trials of Ottoman officials for war crimes including ill-treatment of Armenians during the relocation. These trials were held under the Committee of Union and Progress (CUP) governments during the World War I, the post-CUP governments under British pressure and also in Malta in an unsuccessful operation by the British. The fifth chapter deals with the military motives behind the relocation decision and explains why and how the Ottoman government undertook this troublesome initiative. The role of the Armenian Diaspora in spreading genocide claims is critically examined in the sixth chapter in a way that reveals both the controversies between the Armenian Diaspora and the post-Soviet Republic of Armenia as well as within the Armenian Diaspora itself. Finally, the last chapter analyzes three recent court decisions in Europe questioning the legal validity of both parliamentary resolutions recognizing the Armenian genocide allegations and the presentation of genocide claims as the exclusive truth.

Before elaborating further on the Armenian relocation, it should be noted that to question the existence of genocide is not simply to make prejudicial denial of what the Armenians experienced in 1915. Rather, demystification of the Armenian relocation by reviewing its reasons

It should be noted that to question the existence of genocide is not simply to make prejudicial denial of what the Armenians experienced in 1915. Rather, demystification of the Armenian relocation by reviewing its reasons and consequences requires both sides to eliminate their prejudices.

and consequences requires both sides to eliminate their prejudices. Consequently this study does not intend to devalue what happened to the Ottoman Armenians. It acknowledges the sufferings of the Armenian people throughout the relocation process. However, instead of treating this suffering in isolation, it views it as one of the great tragedies that the peoples of this region experienced in the early twentieth century.

1. The legal definition of genocide

Genocide is a legal concept and, therefore, first and foremost, should be dealt within the context of international law. The universal legal text which establishes whether or not a crime can be defined as genocide is the Genocide Convention. The crime of genocide is defined in the Article 2 of this Convention which provides the most universal definition of this concept. This definition follows as:

In the present Convention, genocide means any of the following acts committed with intent to destroy, in whole or in part, a national, ethnical, racial or religious group, as such:

(a)   Killing members of the group;

(b)   Causing serious bodily or mental harm to members of the group;

(c)   Deliberately inflicting on the group conditions of life calculated to bring about its physical destruction in whole or in part;

(d)   Imposing measures intended to prevent births within the group;

(e)   Forcibly transferring children of the group to another group. (Schabas, 2009, p. 668)

In this article, not only is the crime of genocide defined, but also acts considered to be genocide are clearly identified. Moreover, it is implied that the number of victims is irrelevant except as a strong indication of the seriousness of the crime. In other words, if the elements of genocide mentioned in this article are to be found in a particular case, then regardless of the number of victims that case is to be considered as genocide.

A first glance at the genocidal acts makes a reader inclined to label many incidents in history as genocide, since humanity has witnessed a vast number of mass killings, exterminations, forced prevention of births, or forced transfer of children from one group to another. However, the concept of genocide, being perceived as the "crime of crimes", i.e. the most notorious crime, therefore, its definition has certain limits. There are three expressions in the Article 2, limiting the definition of genocide:

> *The concept of genocide, perceived as the "crime of crimes", i.e. the most notorious crime and, therefore, its definition has certain limits.*

(1) The type of victims: Genocide can only be directed against four types of identified groups, these being national, ethnical, racial or religious groups. Since other social and political groups are excluded from this definition, for instance, the mass killings in the Soviet Union, under Stalin which claimed thousands of lives, could not legally be considered as genocide (Simon, 2007, p. 70).

(2) The intent to destroy: The wording "intent to destroy"

forms the mental or subjective element (*mens rea*) of the crime of genocide. Without the "intent to destroy", no crime can be considered as genocide (Quigley, 2006, pp. 90-91). The intent must be in a special form, in other words, it must either be declared openly (as in the case of the Final Solution decision taken by the Nazi regime at the Wannsee Conference in 1942 [Heller, 2011, p. 283]) or there must be additional evidence (such as the existence of a predetermined extermination plan or an organized group carrying out the genocidal acts in a coordinated, systematic and overwhelming manner) proving the intent to destroy beyond any doubt (Fournet, 2007, p. 63).

Without the "intent to destroy", no crime can be considered as genocide. The intent must be in a special form, in other words, it must either be declared openly or there must be additional evidence proving the intent to destroy beyond any doubt.

(3) The motive to destroy: The wording "as such" denotes the motive of the crime of genocide. It was one of the most debated phrases of the Convention during the preparatory meetings and it limits the scope of the crime of genocide extensively. Accordingly, "as such" means that "[...] only acts aimed at destroying members of one of the four groups, due to no other reason than his or her belonging to that specific group" (Aktan, 2009, p.

141). In other words, motives such as taking revenge, confiscating the victim's possessions or killing a group merely for political reasons may not lead to genocide. As Aktan (2009, p. 141) indicates, "[...] only could a murderously intensive racial hatred towards a group give rise to such a deadly intent".

All in all, for a crime to be labeled as genocide, the three elements mentioned above must be evident. First, the crime should be committed against a particular national, ethnic racial or religious group. Secondly, there should be a clear intent to destroy that can be demonstrated beyond any doubt by evidence. Finally, genocidal acts against a particular group must be perpetrated with a motive of destroying because a person belongs to that specific group. In other words, there must be systematic religious, racial or cultural hatred against that group, evident in the discourse and practical policies of the perpetrators of genocide. Without these three elements (specific groups, intent and motive), naming a particular historical event as genocide would not be legal.

2. The Armenian community in the Ottoman Empire: Was there a racist anti- Armenian discourse in the Ottoman Empire?

If one of the defining elements of genocide is the motive of eliminating a particular group of people solely because they belong to that specific group, then in order to label the 1915 relocation as genocide, one needs to look to see if religious or racial hatred existed against the Armenians living in the Ottoman Empire. Moreover, the Armenian losses experienced during the process of relocation must be in line with this sense of hatred. Answering the following questions enables us to examine the existence or otherwise of a genocidal motive: Was there a racial anti-Armenian discourse and practice in the Ottoman Empire? In other words, did the Ottoman administration perceive the Armenian community as racially inferior, which should be cleansed from Ottoman society? Or, did the Ottoman perception of the Armenians evolve over time in a way, which led to the Armenians being labeled as a specific group to be excluded from the Ottoman multiethnic system?

a. Armenians in the Ottoman Empire's classical period up to the nineteenth century

As a multiethnic and multicultural political entity, the Ottoman Empire perceived the Armenian community as one of the *millets* (religious communities) of the Empire. The *millet* system was based on religious adherence instead of ethnicity. While different Muslim ethnic groups were considered to be members of the same *millet*, non-Muslim communities were divided along religious or sectarian lines (Abu Jaber, 1967, pp. 212-13). For instance, the Greeks and Armenians were considered to be different millets and were organized under different Patriarchates. However, the Bulgarians were considered as being part of the Greek *millet*, because they belonged to the Greek Orthodox Church. Although, by the mid-eighteenth century, the Ottoman documents clearly mention a *millet-i Ermeniyan* (Armenian community), Ottoman institutional policies towards the *millet*s became more systematic only in the mid-nineteenth century after the *Tanzimat* reforms (van der Boogert, 2011, p. 29).

Ottoman treatment of the Armenians was not different from other non-Muslim communities. Their internal affairs were administered by their communal leaders recognized by the state; their formal connection with the Empire was mainly in terms of taxation.

As with other non-Muslim *millet*s, the Armenians were exempted from military service by paying a poll tax (*jizyah*) and a canonical land tax (*haraj*) (Ye'or, 1985, pp. 52-54), until 1839, after which they were still allowed to pay a certain amount of money for being exempted from military service. Moreover, the Armenian Patriarchate was given authority to have jurisdiction over education, social security, the welfare system, religious affairs and family laws of the community. Ottoman treatment of the Armenians was not different from other non-Muslim communities. Their internal affairs were administered by their communal leaders recognized by the state; their formal connection with the Empire was mainly in terms of taxation (Panossian, 2002, p. 128).

The Ottomans clearly trusted Armenians to run important government institutions related to economics and the security of the Empire.

The Armenians of Istanbul were among the most highly esteemed and richest communities of the city. In the eighteenth century in particular the commercial elite of the Armenian community, known as the *amiras*, emerged as the chief money-lenders to the Palace and played a significant role in financing the empire's tax-farming system (Adalian, 2010, p. 216). Moreover, some *amira* families were commissioned to govern some strategic institutions of the Empire. For instance, the Duzian family ruled the imperial mint; the Dadian family administered the imperial gunpowder mill; and some members of the Balian family were appointed as chief architects of the palace (Bournoutian, 2002, p. 190). So the Ottomans clearly trusted Armenians to run important government institutions related to economics and the security of the Empire.

Compared to Istanbul Armenians, Armenians living in Anatolia were more exposed to the instabilities of the Empire's economic and social order. For instance, the Jalali rebellions, which had stormed Anatolia in the seventeenth century, created harsh conditions for all communities the Armenians included. According to Tezcan (2012, p. 204), significant Armenian immigration from Anatolia to Istanbul took place during this period, since they were seeking a safe haven in which they could survive during these rebellions.

Nevertheless, except for minor incidents, there were no inter-communal clashes based on racial or religious hatred. Armenians and other Muslim and non-Muslim elements in the Empire lived together and went through prosperous and critical conditions in exactly the same way.

b. Armenians in the late Ottoman Empire: The nineteenth and early twentieth centuries

If there was no evident racial or religious hatred against the Armenians in the classical age of the Ottoman Empire, was there a systematic sense of enmity based on racial or religious traits in the late Ottoman Empire, where the Armenian national movements began to ascend and inter-communal clashes began to intensify? Historical evidence reveals that, even in the second half of the nineteenth century, when the Eastern question had emerged as a vital problem for the territorial integrity of the Empire, the Ottoman government's perception of Armenians had not acquired a spirit of hatred. For a start the Edict of Reform, adopted in 1856, proclaimed all citizens of the Empire to be equal before law. Although in practice significant problems emerged in achieving legal equality between the Muslim and non-Muslim elements of the Empire, at least theoretically, the Ottoman government declared its intent to eliminate discriminatory policies (Berkes, 1998, pp. 152-153). Secondly, after Greece became independent in 1830, the Armenians began replacing Greeks in Ottoman bureaucracy. There were high-ranking Armenian bureaucrats, parliamentarians, and diplomats serving in the Ottoman bureaucracy (Findley, 1980, 206). Among them were Gabriel Noradoungian, who served as the Ottoman Foreign Minister between 1912 and 1913, Artin Dadian Pasha, who was appointed undersecretary of the Ministry of Foreign Affairs, and Ohannes Sakız Pasha, a close confidant of Abdülhamid II and his Minister for Imperial Treasury (See, Çarkçıyan, 2006). The Ottomans' reliance upon the Armenian bureaucrats is described by Western observers, including an American Minister to Istanbul, who wrote that the Armenian high rank bureaucrats enjoyed equal status with the Muslims: "I have dined out with them [Armenian pashas] at the palace where they sat wearing decorations conferred by the Sultan and mingling on terms of equality with the Mahommedan pashas" (Salt, 2013, p. 55). Ironically, these lines were written when Sultan Abdülhamid II, who was depicted as one of the cruelest Ottoman rulers by the Armenians, was in power.

While Istanbul Armenians largely retained their privileged status, deteriorating economic and social conditions in the countryside continued to adversely affect the Muslim and non-Muslim subjects of the Ottoman Empire. During this period, both the Muslim and non-Muslim subjects were maltreated because of severe economic conditions. So, it would be unfair to claim that only the Armenians were maltreated and that these maltreatments were stemming from religious and racial hatred. Roderic Davison (1963, pp. 116-17) even argues that Christian subjects of the Empire generally enjoyed better conditions compared to the Muslims:

> *"[...] Few Europeans knew or admitted that in many respects the Muslims and Christians suffered equally from brigandage, from corrupt tax collection, or from general misgovernment."*
>
> *Roderic Davison*

[...] Few Europeans knew or admitted that in many respects the Muslims and Christians suffered equally from brigandage, from corrupt tax collection, or from general misgovernment - and that in some instances Christian notables and tax farmers were themselves the oppressors of Muslims. In some ways the Christians were better off than the Turks, since they were exempt from military service and sometimes had foreign consuls to lean on. It was reported from Izmir that "the Turkish villager is, without doubt, more frequently subject to oppression than the Christian". There is evidence to show that in this period there was emigration from independent Greece into the Ottoman Empire, since some Greeks found the Ottoman government a more indulgent master. The sum of the picture is that in many respects all the Ottoman peoples were on the same level, and that the Christian minorities, although of status inferior to the Turks, did not suffer continuously and exclusively from Turkish oppression.

Up to now it has been argued that Armenians were not subjected to systematic racial or religious ill-treatment in the Ottoman classical age as well as in the late Ottoman Empire. The question then becomes: After the Ottoman government encountered Armenian nationalism and Armenian rebellions in both Istanbul and in the countryside, was there a change in its attitude towards the Armenians based on their racial characteristics? Of course, it should be admitted that the Ottoman administration felt significant disappointment over the Armenian rebellions, because they had perceived the Armenians as the "loyal community" of the Empire. During the nineteenth and early twentieth century, many communities in the Ottoman Empire, such as Greeks, Serbs, Wallachians, Moldovans, Bulgarians etc., achieved independence from the Empire, while the Armenians preserved their loyalty until the Ottoman-Russian War of 1877-78 (Libaridian, 2011, p. 74). Even after this war, not all members of the Armenian community strove for independence. However the Armenian rebellions created security problems for the Empire and generally military methods were chosen in response to the rebellions. Nevertheless, Ottoman attitudes towards Armenians who remained loyal had still not changed much. Despite increasing grievances and even rebellions, the Ottoman government continued to employ Armenians in the civil service, even after 1913, when the CUP, often accused of being the perpetrator of the "Armenian genocide", assumed power. For instance, in the 1914-1918 term of the Ottoman Parliament, there were 14 Armenian deputies, who were directly selected by the CUP (Özbudun, 1987, p. 335), men such as Kirkor Zohrab, Onnik

> *Despite increasing grievances and even rebellions, the Ottoman government continued to employ Armenians in bureaucracy, even after 1913, when the CUP, which has been accused for being the perpetrator of the Armenian "genocide", assumed power.*

İhsan, Artin Effendi, Matyos Nalbandyan, Varamyan Effendi, etc (MMZC, 1914). In addition, Oskan Mardikian, an Armenian member of the CUP, was appointed as Minister of Posts and Telegraphs by the CUP administration in January 1913, but resigned in November 1914, because of a political disagreement with the CUP about the entrance of the Ottoman Empire into World War I (Öksüz, 2010, p. 1255).

The CUP also tried to negotiate with the Armenian revolutionary organizations after the eruption of World War I, in order to get their support against the enemies of the Empire (Dündar, 2010, pp. 68-69). Such an attempt at negotiation would have been bizarre, if the CUP members had had a sense of racial or religious hatred towards the Armenians. Finally, not all the Armenian community was relocated in the process of relocation in 1915. For instance, according to an archival document sent by the Office of the Ottoman Chief of Staff to the Commanders of the First, Second and Third Armies, the Armenian families, whose male members were serving in Ottoman military or civil service, should stay where they lived, provided that their numbers locally did not exceed five percent of the total population (BOA DH. EUM. VRK. 15/49, 3 Ağustos 1331 [16 August 1915]). There are also orders from the Ministry of Interior ordering the cancellation of the relocation of Protestant and Catholic Armenians and maintenance of these Armenians in their existing residences (BOA DH. ŞFR, 54-A/290, 23 Temmuz 1331 [5 August 1915] and BOA DH. ŞFR, 55/189, 11 Ağustos 1331 [24 August 1915]). These documents reveal that Armenians were still employed in the Ottoman government service and their families should not be moved. In practice relocation was generally confined to Gregorian Armenians, who were considered to be potential (as well as actual) collaborators with the Russians. In other words, Armenians seemed to have been relocated by the Ottomans not because of their racial or religious traits, but for security reasons, which will be discussed in coming pages.

All in all, the motive for genocidal acts, namely the presence of a sense of racial hatred against a specific group, is an essential element of genocide. In this context, in light of historical evidence, it may be concluded that the argument for the existence of a widespread and systematic racial or religious hatred against the Armenians, leading to their extermination, is highly doubtful. During the Ottoman Empire's classical age, the Armenian community prospered in Istanbul as leading money-lenders, masters of significant governmental posts as well as artisans and craftsmen. Their privileged status continued during the nineteenth century as

Armenians seemed to have been relocated by the Ottomans not because of their racial or religious traits, but for security reasons.

they replaced the Greek-dominated bureaucratic and diplomatic circles. Armenians living in the countryside endured identical conditions with other Muslim and non-Muslim elements of the Empire. They experienced good and wealthy as well as sorrowful and harsh times depending on changing socio-economic and political circumstances. However, it was hardly the case that well-defined governmental ill-treatment of the Armenians took place simply because of their being Armenians. Even, in the late nineteenth and early twentieth century, when the Ottoman government witnessed the rise of Armenian revolutionary movements and rebellions, Ottoman statesmen relied on loyal Armenians. They continued to employ them in government posts. Armenian parliamentarians even served in the Ottoman Parliament during World War I. Hence it is difficult to point to any particular anti-Armenian discourse within the Ottoman Empire, even in the run-up to the events of 1915. So attempts to introduce an artificial narrative, comparable to the anti-Semitic discourse that prevailed in Nazi Germany from early 1930s, are bound to fail.

Even, in the late nineteenth and early twentieth century, when the Ottoman government witnessed the rise of Armenian revolutionary movements and rebellions, Ottoman statesmen relied on loyal Armenians. They continued to employ them in government posts. Armenian parliamentarians even served in the Ottoman Parliament during World War I.

3. Intent to relocate or intent to destroy? Ottoman intentions during the Armenian relocation:

Since genocide is defined as the ultimate crime, one without any equivalent, its definition is restricted by the concept of "intent to destroy". Without the intention to destroy, it would be impossible to define a certain incident causing mass casualties as genocide. As Quigley (2006, p. 29) writes:

> Genocide is distinguished from other serious offenses by the element of intent. For genocide, victimization of human beings is a necessary but not the sole element. Acts directed against human beings must be committed with an intent to destroy a group to which the immediate victims belong. No matter how culpable the actor towards these immediate victims, this additional element is required.

Moreover, Ball (2011, p. 15) argues that according to international law the intent to destroy "must be evident before an action can be labeled genocide." For him, the most significant example of genocidal intent is the Holocaust, before which the intent to destroy the Jews was clear in Nazi administration's official and non-official documentation, including the laws, regulations

The intent to destroy was evident in the case of Holocaust not because the Jews were perceived as a threat to the security or territorial integrity of the Third Reich, but because "for Hitler, the presence of the Jew in Germany despoiled the purity of the Aryan nation, and therefore these "deadly bacilli" had to be destroyed".

and military orders of the Nazi regime as well as Hitler's book *Mein Kampf*. The intent to destroy was evident not because the Jews were perceived as a threat to the security or territorial integrity of the Third Reich, but because "for Hitler, the presence of the Jew in Germany despoiled the purity of the Aryan nation, and therefore these "deadly bacilli" had to be destroyed" (Ball, 2011, p. 15). Moreover, Jews were even brought from remote Greek islands or from the far north of Norway and sent to the concentration camps and hence the internment of Jews was a specific policy which did not exclude any specific segment of the Jewish community.

Of course, it is not easy to discover such explicit evidence of genocidal intent in other cases. Therefore, as several international court decisions indicate, in the absence of direct explicit evidence, genocidal intent must be inferred from circumstantial evidence (Jelisic, ICTY, Trial Judgment, para. 47); however, "that inference must be the only reasonable inference available on the evidence" (Krstic, ICTY, Appellate Judgment, para. 41). Such circumstantial evidence may include:

- The targeting "of a substantial part of the group" (Jelisic, ICTY, Trial Judgment, para. 82),

- "The desired destruction of a more limited number of persons selected [i.e. leadership of the group]" (Jelisic, ICTY, Trial Judgment, para. 82),

- The existence of a plan or policy, although its existence "is not a legal ingredient of genocide" (Jelisic, ICTY, Trial Judgment, para. 48).

It should not be forgotten that these pieces of circumstantial evidence are not *per se* sufficient for labeling an international crime as genocide; but they are supportive elements in the definition of genocide. In the light of these elements, answering the questions below may make it easier to decide whether the Armenian relocation can be considered as genocide or not:

- Was there an open declaration of intent to destroy by the Ottoman government?

- Were the leaders of the Armenian community destroyed during the relocation?

- Was there an organized force to carry out the extermination?

- Was there a predetermined plan of extermination? Was there coordinated, systematic, massive implementation of the genocide?

a. Debates about an open declaration of intent:

To start with the issue of an open declaration of intent to destroy, people labeling 1915 events as genocide generally refers to a group of telegrams, compiled by Aram Andonian and published in 1920 at Paris. These telegrams were generally attributed to the Minister of Interior, Talât Pasha. It is claimed that in these telegrams, Talât Pasha explicitly ordered the extermination of the Armenians.

For instance, in one of these telegrams, dated September 16, 1915, Talât Pasha noted that the CUP had:

decided to destroy completely all the Armenians living in Turkey. Those who oppose this order and decision cannot remain on the official staff of the Empire. An end must be put to their [the Armenians'] existence, however criminal the measure taken may be, and no regard must be paid to either age or sex nor to conscientious scruples. (Lewy, 2005a, p. 58)

The unreliability of Andonian telegrams is not only accepted by Turkish historians, even some authors, who regard the Armenian relocation as genocide, either question the authenticity of these documents or admit that they were compiled for propaganda purposes.

Such an expression would indeed have been perceived as an open declaration of genocidal intent, had these telegrams been authentic. However, it has been unequivocally demonstrated that these telegrams were forged by Andonian as a propaganda tool to convince the Allied Powers of the existence of an intentional extermination of

Armenians (Orel and Yuca, 1986; Gauin, 2011). The unreliability of these telegrams is not only accepted by Turkish historians; even some authors, such as Vahakn Dadrian and Hilmar Kaiser, who regard the Armenian relocation as genocide, either question the authenticity of these documents or admit that they were compiled for propaganda purposes (Lewy, 2005, pp. 63-64). Except for these telegrams, there are other documents, such as the "Ten Commandments of the CUP" or Mevlanzade Rifat's memoirs, which are adduced as proof of the genocidal intent. However, Guenter Lewy (2005a, pp. 43-48) discusses in his book the unreliability of these sources as well. In sum, unlike the Holocaust, until now, the existence of a declaration of genocidal intent by the Ottoman administration has not been clearly proved.

b. Debates about the destruction of the leadership of the Armenian community:

In the absence of open declaration, there might be circumstantial evidences, which could, at least, indicate the genocidal intent. As mentioned above, destroying the leaders of a particular group in a way to make the group defenseless might be perceived as an indication of genocidal intent. Those labeling the 1915 relocation as genocide argue for the arrest and relocation of leaders and members of the Armenian revolutionary organizations as the starting point of genocide. The date of this incident, i.e. 24 April 1915, has even been declared to be the starting date of the "Armenian genocide". There are two antithetical accounts of what really happened on the night of 24 April 1915. These two opposing views agree that hundreds of Armenians (for Sarınay the number is 235 [2008, p. 78]) were arrested in Istanbul with the charge of being members or leaders of Armenian revolutionary organizations, such as the Hinchak, Dashnaksutiun and

Ramgavar, who had been convicted for betraying the Empire and collaborating with Russia and the Allied powers. At the same time, provincial governors were ordered to shut down branches of these Armenian revolutionary organizations in their own provinces and arrest their leaders.

These members or sympathizers of Armenian revolutionary organizations were arrested not because they were Armenian (there were thousands of Armenians living in Istanbul at that time), but because they engaged in revolutionary activities against the government.

From this point on, there are two alternative readings of what had happened in the subsequent period. For those who recognize 1915 relocation as genocide, the aim of these arrests was to destroy the whole Armenian leadership and most of these detainees were massacred by the CUP administration (Melson, 1996, p. 144; Üngör, 2011, p. 67). Those who reject the genocidal intent claim argue that these members or sympathizers of Armenian revolutionary organizations were arrested not because they were Armenian (there were thousands of Armenians living in Istanbul at that time), but because they engaged in revolutionary activities against the government. For Çiçek (2005, p. 35), this charge was clearly stipulated in a British dispatch sent to Admiral

Calthorpe, the British High Commissioner in Istanbul. This dispatch (FO 608/78, 75631, No. 869) mentions that those Armenians who were arrested were either volunteers serving in the Allied armies or perpetrators of massacres against Muslims. These Armenians were sent in the first instance to Ankara and placed in some districts of Ankara province and the district of Çankırı. For instance, in a dispatch sent from the Ministry of Interior to the Governorship of Ankara, dated 25 April 1915, it is mentioned that 180 Armenians were sent to Ankara; these were either leaders of the Armenian revolutionary organizations or persons whose residence in Istanbul were deemed inappropriate. Moreover, the governor was ordered to take necessary precautions for the security of transportation of these Armenians (BOA. DH. ŞFR 52/102, 12 Nisan 1331 [25 April 1915]).

What was the fate of these Armenians? Were they killed by the Ottoman authorities, something which would display the intent to destroy? Ottoman archival documents revealed that some of these Armenians were released to return to Istanbul. For instance, in a dispatch sent to the Governorate of Kastamonu (BOA. DH. ŞFR., 52/255, 24 Nisan 1331 [7 May 1915]), it was ordered that some of the Armenian detainees in Çankırı, such as Gomidas, Vahram Torkumyan, Agob Nargileciyan, Karabet Keropeyan, and others were allowed to return to Istanbul. Another detainee, Dikran Kelekyan, was allowed to reside in a province of his choice other than Istanbul and the provinces heavily populated by Armenians (BOA. DH. ŞFR., 52/266, 25 Nisan 1331 [8 May 1915]). Another group was sent to several provinces for trial by the courts-martial established in these provinces to try the revolutionary activities of the Armenian committees. In these trials, some Armenians were sentenced to death for carrying out assassinations in pursuit of their goals, i.e. an autonomous Armenia, and for their attempts to separate some parts of the Empire. Others were sentenced to various terms of imprisonment or exile to several cities of the Empire (Sarınay, 2012, p. 199). However, the archival documents also show that some of these members of the Armenian elite were killed during the relocation process. For instance, former Ottoman deputies Kirkor Zohrab and Seringulan Vartkes were killed on their transfer to Diyarbakır; however the perpetrators of this crime were tried and sentenced to death by Ottoman martial-law tribunals (Sarınay, 2012, p. 198). Although there were human casualties during the relocation of some of the leaders of the Armenian community of Istanbul, it will be inaccurate to deduce from these casualties that there was an "intent to destroy", given that some of these Armenian community leaders were allowed to return; others were tried and punished in accordance with Ottoman Criminal Law; and, some at least individual Ottoman officials who committed crimes against these Armenians were punished by the courts-martial. To sum up, a genocidal intent to destroy the leadership of the Armenian community is very open to dispute.

c. Debates about the role of the Special Organization in the relocation of the Armenians

A second claim of genocidal intent rests on the nature of relocation as an organized crime, namely, its perpetration by an official secret service organization known as the Special Organization (*Teşkilat-ı Mahsusa*). Historians, who regard the 1915 relocation as genocide, generally accuse this organization of systematically carrying the genocide out on behalf of the government. For instance, Vahakn Dadrian (2004a, p. 236) argues that the Special Organization was established before the relocation and the duty assigned to it was to deploy its agents in remote parts of the

Although there were human casualties during the relocation of some of the leaders of the Armenian community of Istanbul, it will be inaccurate to deduce from these casualties that there was an "intent to destroy", given that some of these Armenian community leaders were allowed to return; others were tried and punished in accordance with Ottoman Criminal Law; and, some at least individual Ottoman officials who committed crimes against these Armenians were punished by the courts-martial.

interior of Anatolia and to ambush and destroy convoys of relocated Armenians. Similarly, Robert Melson (1996, p. 145), writes that "some, if not most, of the massacres were organized by Enver's Special Organization."

Indeed the Special Organization was not established by the CUP. An earlier version of it was first designed by Abdülhamid II as an intelligence organization (Ünlü, 2008, p. 223). Only after 1913 was it renamed the Special Organization and its official duty was to cope with Arab separatism and Western imperialism. For Stoddard, who has written the most extensive book on the activities of the Special Organization, the organization had no direct role in the relocation of Armenians (Stoddard, 1963, pp. 52-58, cited by Lewy, 2005a, p. 73). Other historians such as Jacob Landau, Doğu Ergil, Donald McKale or Eric Jan Zürcher also draw attention to the intelligence and guerilla activities of this organization in the Middle East, North Africa, Caucasus and Central Asia, while they do not focus very much on its role in the Armenian relocation (Lewy, 2005, pp. 73-74).

While Dadrian cites the indictment of the Court Martial of 1919, which put the CUP leaders and Ottoman officials on trial for organizing the massacres of Armenians, as claiming that the Ottoman government used the Special Organization for exterminating the Armenians, Lewy (2005a, p. 77) firmly argues that there is no clear evidence proving that this organization undertook such a notorious mission. Similarly, according to Çiçek (2005, pp. 314-315), most of the sources, which try to link the Special Organization to the Armenian relocation, are the memoirs of those, who had either personal animus against the CUP members or were part of the political alliances established against the CUP. So in his view these memoirs cannot be considered reliable sources bearing in mind the intense hostility between the CUP and its opponents. In sum the alleged role of the Special Organization in the Armenian relocation, namely extermination of Armenians on governmental orders with the intent to destroy, cannot be proved beyond doubt. Hence the suggestion that there was an organization tasked with perpetrating genocide is equally doubtful.

d. Debates about the existence of a systematic plan of extermination before the Armenian relocation

The third piece of circumstantial evidence required for genocidal intent would be the existence of a systematic plan of extermination prepared before the genocidal act. Many historians who regard the events of 1915 as genocide claim that the Ottomans planned the extermination of Armenians long before the relocation. For instance, according to Taner Akçam (2002, p. 167), the CUP became more radical in its policy of Turkification of the Empire especially after the colossal Ottoman defeat in the Balkan Wars. In other words, the CUP leaders decided to eliminate non-Muslim population of the Empire to create a homogenous state. Richard Hovannisian (2007, p. 87) similarly argues for the existence of a systematic plan adopted at a secret meeting of the CUP before the relocation decision. Those historians who question the arguments for genocidal intent claim that the CUP administration had a plan for relocation not extermination, and that even this plan of relocation was not prepared very long before the relocation actually occurred. Grounds for arguing this are as follows:

Historians who question the arguments for genocidal intent claim that the CUP administration had a plan for relocation not extermination, and that even this plan of relocation was not prepared very long before the relocation actually occurred.

First, after the eruption of World War I, the Ottoman administration sought the support of Armenian revolutionary organizations; the series of meetings between Dashnak organization and Ottoman officials continued until August 1914. There are different views with regard to the content of these meetings. While some historians argue that the Armenians did not believe the sincerity of CUP delegates on the issue of reform in the Eastern provinces of the Empire (Gaunt, 2006, pp. 56-57), others claim that the Ottoman administration believed that the Armenian revolutionary organizations had committed an act of betrayal by supporting the Russians against the Empire (Lewy, 2005a, pp. 100-101). However, there is an essential point here that is more important than the content of August 1914 meeting. This is the fact that communication channels between the CUP administration and Dashnak revolutionary organization were still open as late as August 1914. In other words, the suggestion that the Ottoman authorities planned an extermination of Armenians long before the relocation is quite doubtful.

Moreover, both the Temporary Law of Relocation and subsequent decrees on proper administration of the relocation process show that genocidal intent was virtually non-existent. When the text of this law is examined, it will be observed that no ethnic or religious group was targeted. Rather, the first article of the law authorizes the taking of military measures against persons opposing governmental orders, harming the country's defense and the protection of peace. The second article, on the other hand, authorizes military commanders to relocate and resettle people living in villages and towns, individually or in groups, who have been found to be engaged in espionage or treason. Hence the text of the law is clearly defensive (Sarınay, 2012, p. 208). Moreover, subsequent governmental decrees adopted for the proper administration of the relocation show that the ultimate intention of the government was not the destruction of Armenians. These decrees include following provisions (Sarınay, 2012, p. 208):

> *Subsequent governmental decrees adopted for the proper administration of the relocation show that the ultimate intention of the government was not the destruction of Armenians.*

- The security of relocated Armenians should be ensured; if possible, they should be relocated by available transportation facilities.

- The daily subsistence requirements of the relocated Armenians should be met.

- Once relocated, Armenians should be provided with properties and fields corresponding to their financial and economic conditions prior to relocation.

- The government should provide Armenians in need with shelter.

- The farmers, artisans and craftsmen among the relocated Armenians should be provided with seeds and equipment of their profession.

The properties left by the relocated Armenians posed a significant problem for the Ottoman administration. Historians, who recognize the 1915 incidents as genocide, claim that the Turkish administration confiscated all properties of the Armenians since the real intent was to exterminate whole Armenian community (see, for instance, Akçam and Kurt, 2012). On the other hand, historians disputing the genocidal intent argument claim that the "abandoned properties" (*emvâl-i metruke*) of relocated Armenians were clearly recorded and administered through a decree approved on 10 June 1915. According to that decree, commissions would be established to hold the records of the abandoned goods, to administer the sale of these properties by auction, and to preserve the revenues obtained from these sales on behalf of the relocated Armenians (Sarınay, 2012, p. 241). These decrees on the proper administration of relocation and abandoned goods indicate that the government hardly acted with the intent to destroy.

e. Debates about the inappropriate conditions during the Armenian relocation

Another argument concerning genocidal intent relates to the inappropriate conditions of the final destinations of relocation and the method of transportation. Accordingly, historians arguing the existence of an "Armenian genocide" claim that the Ottomans forced the

Armenians into a "death march" in order to annihilate them. The final destination of this "death march" was a desert where conditions were extremely unfavorable for survival (Thompson, 2013, p. 120).

It should be admitted that the relocation process was not easy. Hundred thousands of people were moved without any proper means of transport. Some of them failed to reach the ultimate destination of the relocation operation either because of the spread of lethal diseases or the lack of proper alimentation. Moreover, some of them were killed either by irregular bands or sometimes on the orders of officials who had acted against governmental decrees ordering the provision of security of the relocated Armenians. In other words, while the Ottoman administration tried to prevent such casualties, under war-time conditions, it largely failed. However, the mass casualties experienced during the relocation were not an outcome of a genocidal intent. As Çiçek (2010, pp. 121-122) writes, in order to ameliorate the conditions for the relocated Armenians, the government allocated a certain amount of daily allowance for them (1 piaster for adults and 20 paras for children according to an American eyewitness) and allowed international relief organizations such as Red Cross and American Committee for Armenian and Syrian Relief to help them (Lewy, 2005a, pp. 194-195). Moreover, not all of the Armenians were settled in the tent camps established near the Euphrates. Where they were available, the government tried to resettle relocated Armenians in proper houses in several towns and cities, such as Damascus, Aleppo, Ma'an, Ras-al Ayn, etc (Çiçek, 2010, p. 122). Hence, although the government could not manage the process of relocation without casualties, its intention seems to have been not to destroy but to resettle the Armenians.

All in all, the intent to destroy is the essence of the crime of genocide, without which any incident cannot be regarded as genocide. As discussed above, up to now, no official Ottoman document stipulating, beyond any doubt, that the Armenian community of the Empire suffered losses because they were Armenian, has ever been discovered in the archives. The circumstantial evidence

> *Up to now, no official Ottoman document stipulating, beyond any doubt, that the Armenian community of the Empire suffered losses because they were Armenian, has ever been discovered in the archives.*

also falls short of fulfilling the criteria for genocidal intent. It was not the leaders of the Armenian community who were arrested and tried but mostly the members of the Armenian revolutionary organizations, people who were convicted for attempting to create an autonomous Armenia in a way that violated the territorial integrity of the Empire. Although some were sentenced to death, this was not because of their ethnic or religious origin, but because of their political affiliations, which were a crime punishable by death under the existing criminal code of the Empire. Some of these detainees were also released. While these arrests were being held in Istanbul, more than 70.000 Armenians in the city were not relocated and continued with their lives. Even, for Çiçek (2010, p. 125), by late July 1917, when the CUP was still in power, there were 522 Armenians employed in Ottoman bureaucracy. Other necessary pieces of circumstantial evidence, such as the role of the Special Organization or the existence of a predetermined plan of annihilation, do not have a clear existence. Many historians cannot discern any link between the Special Organization and the Armenian casualties as mentioned above. Moreover, one of the reasons for the Armenian casualties during the relocation process seems to be the lack of a predetermined plan of relocation rather than the existence of one. In other words, the Ottoman administration could not manage and allocate enough resources for the relocation process. Although, the administration tried to minimize casualties through governmental decrees, the losses of relocated Armenians were still high. However, this does not mean definitely that the Ottoman government acted with genocidal intent.

4. Trials of Ottoman officials for war crimes including the ill-treatment of Armenians

The Armenian relocation was not an easy process; certainly there was significant Armenian suffering during relocation. As mentioned in the previous sections, some of this suffering occurred because of the difficulties of the process of relocation itself. Transferring hundred thousands of people in hot summertime with inadequate transport facilities and without proper alimentation caused diseases to spread and led to significant casualties on the way. But, more important than that, the relocated Armenians were occasionally attacked by irregular bands. They were ill-treated by some governmental officials, and the property of some Armenians was illegally confiscated or looted during the process of relocation. In other words, in addition to the natural causes of casualties resulting from the inability of the government to administer the relocation process properly, several crimes were committed against the relocated Armenians.

a. Two opposing views of the courts-martial

Historians, who accept that the 1915 events were genocide, have perceived these crimes committed against the relocated Armenians as a strong indication of genocidal intent. They draw attention to these crimes by some Ottoman officials and argue that they were systematically sponsored by the government. Hence the casualties of the relocation demonstrate a strong intent to destroy. These historians also lay a specific emphasis on the 1919-1920 courts-martial, which tried and punished the CUP leaders and many members of this party for war crimes, including those that had been committed against the Armenians during relocation. According to these historians, the proceedings and verdicts of these courts-martial prove the genocidal intent of the CUP government (For instance, Dadrian and Akçam, 2011, pp. 1-2; Winter, 2003, p. 211; Melson, 1996, p. 152). Moreover, they claim that the 1919-1920 courts-martial might also be recognized as a "competent tribunal" to try and punish the crime of genocide, as stipulated in the Article 6 of the Convention, which follows as:

> Persons charged with genocide or any of the other acts enumerated in Article III shall be tried by a competent tribunal of the State in the territory of which the act was committed, or by such international penal tribunal as may have jurisdiction with respect to those Contracting Parties which shall have accepted its jurisdiction. (Schabas, 2009, p. 668)

By contrast historians, who deny the genocidal intent argument, claim that there are two shortcomings in this point of view. First, the perception of the 1919-1920 courts-martial as competent tribunals is quite controversial, since these courts were established under the pressure of Allied powers after the end of the World War I in an occupied Istanbul. Many Western observers even doubted the impartiality of the courts and the reliability of their verdicts. Secondly, and more importantly, the advocates of genocidal intent generally ignore another set of courts-martial established in 1916, when the CUP was still in power, to try and punish persons who had committed several crimes including the ill-treatment of the relocated Armenians and illegal confiscation of their properties. In other words, it would be extremely paradoxical to claim that the CUP had a genocidal intent to exterminate all the Armenians while courts-martial, established by the CUP, tried and punished persons who had ill-treated the relocated Armenians.

The advocates of genocidal intent generally ignore another set of courts-martial established in 1916, when the CUP was still in power, to try and punish persons who had committed several crimes including the ill-treatment of the relocated Armenians and illegal confiscation of their properties.

b. The 1916 Courts-Martial: A CUP attempt to try the culprits:

The CUP administration became aware of ill treatment and even massacres of Armenians at the outset of the relocation process. There are many documents in the Ottoman archives, demonstrating that the government tried to prevent and punish the ill-treatment of Armenians. For instance, in a dispatch Minister of Interior, Talât Pasha sent to the governor's office in Urfa, there is mention of some gendarmes who had accompanied a group of relocated Armenians and then allowed irregular bands to capture some of the Armenian women. Talât Pasha ordered the governor very clearly to send these gendarmes to a court-martial for trial and punishment (Çiçek, 2005, p. 211). Similarly, in another dispatch (BOA. DH. ŞFR, 54-A/348, 28 R 1333 [9 August 1915]) sent to the governor of Gümüşhane, it was mentioned that the inspector of the CUP in the city of Mamüret-ül Aziz had confiscated some Armenian properties for his own benefit. Again, the governor was ordered to send the inspector to the court-martial for trial and punishment. Such documents reveal that the government intended to prevent the illegal transfer of property as well as ill-treatment of relocated Armenians rather than intending to destroy them.

There are many documents in the Ottoman archives, demonstrating that the government tried to prevent and punish the ill-treatment of Armenians.

In addition to these individual investigations, as a response to increasing intelligence on the crimes committed against the Armenians, on 30 September 1915, the government decided to send inquiry commissions to the relocation regions to investigate abuses and misconduct by Ottoman officials (Sarınay, 2012, p. 247). These inquiry commissions identified 1673 people (528 government officials, 170 local officials, and 975 civilians) accused of alleged crimes against the relocated Armenians and sent them to the courts-martial. They were tried for charges such as murder, rape, wounding, bribery, forced confiscation, harming Armenian properties, illegal marriages with Armenian women, and misconduct. As a result of the trials, which continued until the mid-1916, 67 individuals were sentenced to death; 524 individuals were sentenced to imprisonment; and 68 individuals were sentenced to exile, penal servitude, or a judicial fine (Sarınay, 2012, pp. 248-50). Thus, at least some culprits were punished by the Ottoman judiciary when the CUP was still in power. This also casts a shadow on the argument of genocidal intent.

c. The 1919-20 Courts-Martial and the Malta investigations:

The 1916 courts-martial were not sufficient; even Talât Pasha himself admitted in his memoirs that not all the perpetrators of massacres or maltreatment of Armenians could be tried and punished (Lewy, 2005a, p. 114). Therefore, when World War I ended and the Allied powers began occupying several parts of the Ottoman Empire after the Armistice of Mudros, the Allied powers forced the new Ottoman government to try and punish the perpetrators of the Armenian relocation. As a result, by the late 1918, an inquiry commission was established to investigate crimes against Armenians and this commission prepared files for the trial of several

CUP leaders as well as members of former governments (Akçam, 2002, pp. 453-54). This was followed by the establishment of a court-martial in December 1918. This tribunal started investigations; however, the new Grand Vizier, Damad Ferid Pasha, considered the procedure of the court to be extremely slow. In order to appease the British, he abolished it and set up a new one to accelerate the legal procedures. However, the members of this new tribunal felt themselves under strong governmental and external pressure and most of them resigned during the trials (Ata, 2005, pp. 133-35). Under this pressure, the court speeded up the process and the sentences were proclaimed and carried out immediately.

Meanwhile, the most significant trial, namely the trial of the leaders and prominent members of the CUP started in April 1919. The triumvirate and some leading cadres of the CUP had left the country and their trials were conducted in absentia. However for others arrested by British intervention, no clear evidence proving their role in the Armenian massacres could be found. Still, a district governor of Boğazlıyan, Kemal Bey, was declared guilty and sentenced to death. His execution caused significant public outrage against the government and the British. Therefore, the British authorities decided to transfer the trial of CUP leaders to their own territory. They intervened and transferred prominent members of the CUP to Malta for trial (Ata, 2005, p. 220). However, at the end of the investigations, the Chief Crown Prosecutor declared that no clear evidence could be found to accuse the detainees in Malta of perpetrating mass massacres against the Armenians during the relocation, and there was therefore no need for further prosecution (Şimşir, 2009, p. 289).

The CUP leaders, who had left the country, were continued facing charges in the Istanbul court-martial. Finally, the tribunal decided to pass death sentences *in absentia* on Talât Pasha, Cemal Pasha, Enver Pasha, Dr. Nazım Bey and Bahaeddin Şakir. After Istanbul was officially occupied by the Allied troops on 16 March 1920, under extreme British pressure, Damad Ferid Pasha forced the courts-martial to give their decisions immediately. As a result, several government officials were sentenced to death and the sentences were carried out as well (Ata, 2005, pp. 260-72).

> *At the end of the Malta investigations, the Chief Crown Prosecutor declared that no clear evidence could be found to accuse the detainees in Malta of perpetrating mass massacres against the Armenians during the relocation.*

The 1919-1920 courts-martial produced a controversial literature. On the one hand, some historians regard these courts as reliable judicial mechanisms proving the genocidal intent of the government (Dadrian, 2004b,

p. 1); on the other hand, other historians discussed the extreme intervention by the Allied powers in the judicial process and the lack of objectivity in the judges, whom were known for their hatred against the CUP regime (Ata, 2005, p. 115). For instance, according to Feridun Ata, Sultan Mehmed VI Vahideddin demanded the establishment of tribunals having extraordinary powers not for fair trial of the perpetrators of crimes against the Armenians, but to relieve Allied pressure on the state. The Sultan believed that ordinary courts require lengthy processes of investigation and prosecution, while the Europeans were extremely impatient to have the CUP members punished (Ata, 2004, p. 310). Moreover, one of

Moreover, one of the presiding judges of these courts, Mustafa Pasha, stated clearly that "a court-martial operating under occupation acts in line with emotions instead of conscience. This is an order coming from above".

the presiding judges of these courts, Mustafa Pasha, stated clearly that "a court-martial operating under occupation acts in line with emotions instead of conscience. This is an order coming from above" (Ata, 2004, p. 322). Such a declaration demonstrates the lack of impartiality in these courts.

The judgments of these courts were put under closer examination in November 1920 by the new government established by Tevfik Pasha. The right to appeal, which had not been previously permitted, was given to those convicted in the 1919-1920 courts-martial. The Military Court of Appeal investigated the decisions taken by these courts-martial and discovered significant inconsistencies and improprieties in them. Almost all the judgments made by the courts-martial after 23 April 1920 were reversed in this Court of Appeal (Sarınay, 2012, p. 257). It should be noted that these decisions on reversing the judgment were taken when Istanbul was still under Allied occupation. The Allied Powers did not react to this development, since even they were not convinced that the judgments of the 1919-1920 courts-martial were reliable. For instance, Lewis Heck, the U.S.

> *"It is popularly believed that many of [the trials] are made from motives of personal vengeance or at the instigation of the Entente authorities, especially the British". Lewis Heck, the U.S. High Commissioner in Istanbul.*

High Commissioner in Istanbul, reported, "it is popularly believed that many of [the trials] are made from motives of personal vengeance or at the instigation of the Entente authorities, especially the British" (Lewy, 2005b). As Lewy (2005b) writes clearly:

> At the time, the victorious Allies considered them a travesty of justice. The trials, British high commissioner S.A.G. Calthorpe wrote to London, are "proving to be a farce and injurious to our own prestige and to that of

the Turkish government." In the view of Commissioner John de Robeck, the tribunal was such a failure "that its findings cannot be held of any account at all."

All in all, the trials of the perpetrators of crimes against the Armenians hardly demonstrate any genocidal intent. On the one hand, there were 1916 courts-martial; they were established by the CUP accused of being the perpetrator of the "Armenian genocide." These courts-martial had tried hundreds of people and punished some of them for the crimes they had committed against the relocated Armenians. On the other hand, there were the 1919-1920 courts-martial, established under great pressure from the Allied Powers who had threatened the Sultan and the government to formally occupy Istanbul. Trial procedures were not appropriate. There were false witnesses; exaggerated testimony; a prejudiced presiding judge, who acted as a prosecutor instead of an impartial judge, and so forth. Of course, the structural problems of these courts (1919-20 courts-martial) do not necessarily mean that no crimes had been committed against the Armenians by Ottoman officials. The claim here is simply that these courts cannot be described as a competent national court for the trial of the crime of genocide as stipulated in the Article 6 of the Convention and their verdicts do not prove that there was any genocidal intent.

5. Relocation as a military precaution?

The process of relocation of Armenians in 1915 was quite awkward. Thousands of Armenians were given a short period of time to prepare; they were forced to leave their homes and to head towards a destination unknown to them. The journey was long and conditions were hard. During the hot summer days, a number of the luckier Armenians were transported by trains. Others had to walk long distances. Epidemics were widespread. Alimentation was not sufficient, and security for the convoys could not be adequately provided. Moreover, the conditions at the final destination of the relocation, namely in the Syrian provinces of the Ottoman Empire, were also not appropriate. Attempts were made to settle the Armenians in city centers. However, most of them had to stay in tents in camps established near the Euphrates. Hence casualties among the relocated Armenians were severe.

Why then did the Ottoman administration choose to arrange for the relocation of Armenians in the midst of a fierce war with the Allied powers? Why did the government engage in this costly mass transfer of Armenians, whom they had earlier labeled as the "loyal nation"? Why did the Ottoman policy makers decide to allocate significant financial resources for the organization of relocation at the end of which severe casualties would be inevitable? Did the Ottoman administration really intend to destroy the Armenian nation? If so, how does one explain facts such as the thousands of Armenians, who were not relocated, the hundreds of Armenian governmental employees, who worked in Ottoman diplomatic and bureaucratic circles even during World War I, and the hundreds of Ottoman officials, who were tried and punished for the ill-treatment of Armenians during the relocation? If there was no intent to destroy, what was the real intention behind such an extraordinarily difficult operation?

a. Military motives of the Armenian relocation

The real intention behind the Armenian relocation was military necessity. In other words, the Armenian relocation was a military precaution.

According to those historians who oppose the "genocidal intent" argument the real intention behind the Armenian relocation was military necessity. In other words, the Armenian relocation was a military precaution. This point of view rests on the argument that by the end of the nineteenth century, the newly established Armenian revolutionary organizations began agitating among the Armenian population for an independent Armenia. Supported mainly by the Russians, these revolutionary organizations employed aggressive methods, including armed resistance, against the Ottoman Empire. There was a brief period of peace between these organizations and the Ottoman administration after the restoration of the

Ottoman constitution in 1908, but after the loss of the Balkan Wars and particularly with the outbreak of World War I, some Armenian revolutionary organizations began cooperating with the Russians, the main adversary of the Ottoman Empire in Eastern Anatolia. To forestall this cooperation and also atrocities committed by Armenians against the Muslim population of the region, the Ottoman government decided to relocate the Armenians to the regions far away from the Russian front. Hence the idea of relocation emerged as a military precaution (Uras, 1987, pp. 571-578; Sonyel, 1993, pp. 280-307; Erickson, 2011, pp. 291-298).

The mentality of multiethnic empires in the age of nationalism has to be taken into consideration in order to understand the motives behind the relocation. Accordingly, the nationalist movements, inspired by the French revolution, severed the relations between the center and periphery of the multiethnic empires. Peoples in the periphery began to define themselves as a nation and to strive to achieve political targets ranging from basic political rights to full independence. The response of conservative monarchies to these demands was mixed. Most of the European monarchies were grouped within the Concert of Europe, established in 1815 after the Napoleonic wars, and they decided to cooperate against nationalist and liberal political movements including the claims for independence (Chapman, 1998, p. 83). They tried to suppress these movements by force as was evident in the cases of Hungarian and Polish rebellions against the Austro-Hungarian Empire (Roessler and Miklos, 2003, p. 147) and Caucasian rebellions against the Russian Empire (King, 2008, pp. 77-91). Since agreement existed among the European powers to help each other in suppressing rebellions for independence, the European response to these bloody reprisals was generally total silence.

The Ottoman case was quite different. The Ottomans were not part of the Concert of Europe until 1856. Hence the earliest independence movements within the Empire after 1815 were not perceived by the Europeans as being similar to the independence movements experienced in Europe. For instance, the Greek War of Independence was actively supported by the European powers; a joint fleet of Britain, France and Russia even attacked and burned the Ottoman fleet at the Bay of Navarino in 1827. Although the Ottoman Empire perceived this independence movement as a vital threat to itself and tried to suppress it by every means it could, the European powers sided openly with the Greeks, and considered them to be an oppressed nation deserving the right to independence (Clogg, 2013, pp. 39-45). This policy, considered hypocritical, disappointed the Ottoman Empire.

The Greek War of Independence turned out to be a model for the other nations of the Empire. The Serbian uprisings ended first with autonomy and then with independence.

Romanian revolutionary activities soon culminated in autonomy and independence as well (Nicolaidis, 2011 p. 169). The methods employed by these nations were generally identical. First they incited a small rebellion and waited the Ottoman administration to respond militarily. Afterwards this military response was depicted as a massacre of Christian nations by the Ottoman Empire, and attempts were made to rouse European public opinion. Then the European powers intervened forcing the Ottoman Empire to engage in a policy of reform, which first led to autonomy. Once autonomy was granted the road to independence was opened. Finally, when the conditions were appropriate, a declaration of independence was proclaimed. This proclamation was made either after a significant Ottoman military defeat or after a vital political transformation. For instance, Greek independence was granted after the Ottoman-Russian War of 1828-29. The Serbians, Romanians and Montenegrins achieved full independence after the Ottoman-Russian War of 1877-78. Bulgaria declared its independence after the restoration of the Ottoman Constitution in 1908, and finally Albania became officially independent after the Balkan Wars of 1912-13. At the end of the Balkan

> *The Greek War of Independence turned out to be a model for the other nations of the Empire. The Serbian uprisings ended first with autonomy and then with independence. Romanian revolutionary activities soon culminated in autonomy and independence as well.*

Wars, Armenians were the largest non-independent Christian community in the Empire. However, from the late nineteenth century onwards, they were aware of this pattern of independence.

b. Activities of Armenian revolutionary organizations

Inspired by the nationalist fervor of the French revolution and learning from the patterns of independence of other Christian communities of the Ottoman Empire, certain number of the Armenians began striving for independence from the Empire.

As mentioned above, historians denying a genocidal intention behind the Armenian relocation base their arguments on the existence of separatist Armenian revolutionary movements and on the rebellions ignited by them since the late nineteenth century. Inspired by the nationalist fervor of the French revolution and learning from the patterns of independence of other Christian communities of the Ottoman Empire, certain number of the Armenians began striving for independence from the Empire. The turning point was the Ottoman-Russian War of 1877-78. Toward the end of the war, the Armenian Patriarch of Istanbul, Nerses Varjabedian, contacted Tsar Alexander

II of Russia via the Catholicos of Etchmiadzin, and demanded that Russia should not to return Eastern Anatolia under occupation by Russian forces to the Ottoman Empire. In his correspondence with him, Varjabedian asked the Russian Commander, Grand Duke Nicholas to annex Eastern Anatolia and to establish an autonomous Armenian state there under Russian tutelage (Adalian, 2010, p. 583). This demand could not be fulfilled because the Treaty of Berlin later reversed most of the Russian gains in the Treaty of St. Stefano. The Russians restored Eastern Anatolia to the Ottoman Empire on condition that the Ottomans had to engage in reforms in the Eastern provinces of the Empire. However, the Ottomans fully grasped the meaning of a "reform" which would ultimately lead to autonomy followed by independence. Hence they dragged their feet in making the required reforms in the Eastern provinces (Karsh and Karsh, 2001, pp. 152-153).

The Armenian Patriarch failed to achieve what he had wanted. Indeed, what he had in mind was the creation of an autonomous Armenia under Russian patronage rather than full independence. However, the Ottoman-Russian war inspired more secular Armenians to establish an independent state in the region to be called Greater Armenia. So from early 1880s onwards, Armenian revolutionary committees began to be founded. The first initiative was a clandestine group, known as the "Defenders of the Homeland" established in Erzurum province and dedicated to the purchase of weapons and military training for resisting against the Ottoman administration (Erickson, 2013, p. 10). Soon after this original initiative, the Armenakan Party was founded as the first Armenian political party aimed at winning "for the Armenians the right to rule over themselves through revolution" (Erickson, 2013, p. 11). In other words, from the beginning independence was the goal and revolution the method. According to Louise Nalbandian (1963, p. 101), "[...] certain episodes indicate that the Armenakans did not stop at mere defensive action, but also incited trouble and committed terroristic acts."

The Ottoman-Russian war of 1877-78 inspired more secular Armenians to establish an independent state in the region to be called Greater Armenia. So, from early 1880s onwards, Armenian revolutionary committees began to be founded.

It was not very difficult for the Ottoman government to suppress the Armenakan Party and as a result of government pressure, the party soon went underground. Fearing the Ottoman response, new political parties such as Hinchak and the Dashnaksutiun (the Armenian Revolutionary Federation, or Dashnak Party) were established in Geneva in 1887 and in Tbilisi in 1890, respectively. From the very beginning, these two parties were structured as revolutionary organizations aimed at independence to be achieved via armed resistance and terror. The program of the Hinchak Party clearly emphasized that "the immediate objective of the party was the political and national independence of Turkish Armenia" (Nalbandian, 1963, p. 108). In pursuit of this ultimate aim, agitation and terror were considered significant methods:

Agitation and terror we needed to "elevate the spirit" of the people... The people were also to be incited against their enemies and were to "profit" from retaliatory actions of these same enemies. Terror was to be used as a method of protecting the people and winning their confidence in the Hinchak program. The party aimed at terrorizing the Ottoman government, thus contributing toward lowering the prestige of that regime and working toward its complete disintegration. The government itself was not to be the only focus of terroristic tactics. The Hinchaks wanted to annihilate the most dangerous of the Armenian and Turkish individuals who were then working for the government as well as to destroy all spies and informers. To assist them in carrying out all of these terroristic acts, the party was

> *The [Hinchak] party aimed at terrorizing the Ottoman government, thus contributing toward lowering the prestige of that regime and working toward its complete disintegration. The government itself was not to be the only focus of terroristic tactics. The Hinchaks wanted to annihilate the most dangerous of the Armenian and Turkish individuals who were then working for the government as well as to destroy all spies and informers.*
>
> *Louise Nalbandian*

to organize an exclusive branch specifically devoted to performing acts of terrorism. (Nalbandian, 1963, p. 110)

Moreover according to the Hinchak party program, "the most opportune time to institute the general rebellion for carrying out immediate objectives was when Turkey was engaged in war" (Nalbandian, 1963, p. 111). World War I would later be perceived as this "most opportune time" for a general rebellion against the Ottoman Empire.

The Dashnaksutiun had similar targets and methods. In its party program, it was clearly stated that the party's aim was "to bring about the political and economic freedom of Turkish Armenia by means of rebellion" (Nalbandian, 1963, p. 167). The methods used to achieve this aim, included establishing war bands, using every means to arm the people, organizing revolutionary committees, stimulating conflict and terrorizing government officials and "traitors", establishing communications for the transportation of men and arms (Nalbandian, 1963, p. 168).

In sum, these organizations were not simple political parties: they were revolutionary organizations with a single objective - achieving independence from the Ottoman Empire. Moreover their methods were not peaceful. Methods like agitation, terror, or massive armament demonstrated that these parties would create security problems for the Ottoman Empire from the outset. Indeed, demonstrations, rebellions, and armed attacks against the Ottoman officials began soon after the establishment of these revolutionary organizations.

The first revolt came at Erzurum in 1890. It was followed by the Kumkapı riots in Istanbul the same year, and then by uprisings in Kayseri, Yozgat, Çorum and Merzifon in 1892-93, in Sasun in 1894, the Zeytoun revolt and the Armenian raid on the Sublime Porte in 1895, the Van revolt and occupation of the Ottoman Bank in Istanbul in 1896, the Second Sasun revolt in 1903, the attempted assassination of Sultan Abdulhamid II in 1905, and the Adana revolt in 1909. The main aim of these revolts was to attract a fierce governmental response and then present the Armenian casualties as massacres of Armenians by the Ottoman administration. This aim was clearly stated in the writings of European diplomats serving in the Ottoman Empire. For instance, in his dispatch to the Foreign Office, dated 28 March 1894,

> *These organizations were not simple political parties; they were revolutionary organizations with a single objective achieving independence from the Ottoman Empire. Moreover their methods were not peaceful. Methods like agitation, terror, or massive armament demonstrated that these parties would create security problems for the Ottoman Empire from the outset.*

the British ambassador in Istanbul, Sir Philip Currie, wrote "the aim of the Armenian revolutionaries is to stir disturbances, to get the Ottomans to react to violence, and thus get the foreign powers to intervene" (Heper and Criss, 2009, p. 19).

The pattern of independence already mentioned seems to have been at work. The Ottoman government usually sent armed forces to suppress the rebellions and crushed the revolutionaries, as a result of which a number of innocent Armenians were sometimes killed during the clashes. Armenian casualties were immediately reported as massacres of Armenians by the Ottomans and European states pressed the government to halt the massacres and engage in reforms in Eastern Anatolia.

"The aim of the Armenian revolutionaries is to stir disturbances, to get the Ottomans to react to violence, and thus get the foreign powers to intervene."
Sir Philip Currie, the British Ambassador to the Port (1894).

The separatist policies of the Armenian revolutionary organizations seemed to diminish with the restoration of the Ottoman constitution in 1908. The Armenians and the Ottomans were both hopeful that peaceful coexistence might be possible within a parliamentary monarchy

(Sonyel, 1993, pp. 295-296). However in the following years neither side was satisfied with the course of events. The Armenians were disappointed that the government did not engage in the reforms promised in the Treaty of Berlin. The Ottomans were disappointed too because they perceived that the Armenians had already achieved significant rights. There were even Armenian deputies elected to articulate the problems of the Armenian people. Therefore there was no need for further reform and any demands for reform might ultimately imply demands for autonomy and independence.

c. Ottoman-Armenian relations on the eve of the World War I and before the Armenian relocation

This mutual distrust between the Ottoman administration and the Armenian revolutionary organizations grew worse after the Balkan Wars. These wars were a massive trauma for the Ottomans. The loss of all the Empire's Balkan territories to the small Balkan states which till then had been part of the Ottoman Empire, caused fear of further secessions from the Empire (Akçam, 2004, pp. 94-95). The Balkan Wars intensified a sense of insecurity throughout the Empire as well. In particular the Eastern provinces witnessed increasing inter-communal clashes between Armenians and Kurds, as a result of which both communities attempted to upgrade their military capacity. For instance, the Dashnaks sent representatives to Tekirdağ province in Eastern Thrace to purchase rifles in huge quantities, because in Thrace after the Balkan Wars, there was an abundance of military weapons (Erickson, 2013, p. 106).

Moreover by the end of 1913, the Armenian revolutionary organizations were aware that a great war was imminent between the Ottomans and the Russians. In their congresses, which had taken place in 1913, contradictory policies emerged in different committees. While the Dashnaks decided to support the Ottoman Empire in a prospective war without preventing the Russian Armenians from supporting Russia, the Hinchaks decided covertly to return to the use of violence to achieve their political aims (Erickson, 2013, p. 109). Papazian (1934, p. 38), on the other hand, writes that the Dashnaks were not sincere in their pledge of support towards the Ottoman Empire in the coming war, namely the World War I:

"The leaders of the Turkish-Armenian section of the Dashnagtzoutune did not carry out the promise of loyalty to the Turkish cause when the Turks entered the war."

Kapriel Serope Papazian

> The leaders of the Turkish-Armenian section of the Dashnagtzoutune did not carry out the promise of loyalty to the Turkish cause when the Turks entered the war... They were swayed in their actions by the

interests of the Russian government, and disregarded, entirely, the political dangers that the war had created for the Armenians in Turkey. Prudence was thrown to the winds: even the decision of their own convention of Erzurum was forgotten, and a call was sent for Armenian volunteers to fight the Turks on the Caucasian front.

Similarly, Kachaznouni (1955, p. 1) clearly mentions that the Dashnaks acted contrary to the pledge they gave to the Ottomans at the Erzurum meeting of August 1914 and sided with the Russians during the World War I:

"Contrary to the decision taken during their general meeting at Erzeroum only a few weeks before, the A.R.F. had active participation in the formation of the bands and their future military action against Turkey."

Hovhannes Kachaznouni

At the beginning of the fall of 1914 when Turkey had not yet entered the war but had already been making preparations, Armenian revolutionary bands began to be formed in Transcaucasia with great enthusiasm and, especially, with much uproar. Contrary to the decision taken during their general meeting at Erzeroum only a few weeks before, the A.R.F. had active participation in the formation of the bands and their future military action against Turkey.

In sum, it was evident that the eruption of World War I seemed to be just the opportunity for which the Armenian revolutionary organizations had waited for so long. By supporting the Russians against the Ottomans, they tried to achieve independence under Russian auspices. Among the Ottoman Armenians serving the Russians, there were former members of the Ottoman Parliament, such as Armen Garo (Karekin Pastırmadjiyan) and Murad (Hamparsum Boyadjian). Dashnaks soon began to gather Armenian volunteers to serve for the Russian army. Hundreds of volunteers were convened under the Armenian military leader Antranik, who led an Armenian legion, composed of 1200 men deployed to the Persian border. Other Armenian legions were stationed on the Ottoman-Russian borders in order to attack the Ottoman forces (Erickson, 2013, p. 145). When the Ottoman armies attempted to recapture territories lost during the 1877-78 Ottoman-Russian War, these Armenian legions supported the Russian army and contributed to the Russian victory against the Ottoman Empire (Erickson, 2013, p. 145).

The belligerent position of the Ottoman Armenians was outlined very clearly by Boghos Nubar Pasha, head of the Armenian delegation at the Paris Peace Conference after World War I. In a letter addressed to the French Foreign Minister, Boghos Nubar wrote as follows:

> Dear Minister,
>
> I have the honor, in the name of the Armenian National Delegation, of submitting to Your Excellency the following declaration, at the same time reminding that: The Armenians have been, since the beginning

of the war, de facto belligerents, as you yourself have acknowledged, since they have fought alongside the Allies on all fronts, enduring heavy sacrifices and great suffering for the sake of their unshakeable attachment to the cause of the Entente.

...

In the Caucasus, where, without mentioning the 150.000 Armenians in the Imperial Russian Army, more than 40.000 of their volunteers contributed to the liberation of a portion of the Armenian vilayets [...] (Feigl, 1986, pp. 102-103)

In other words, Boghos Nubar Pasha was saying that the Armenians did not remain loyal citizens of the Empire. They rose up against it and fought alongside the Allies. They were faithful allies of the Entente powers experiencing severe losses as a result. These words demonstrate that the security problem created by Armenian committees was not imaginary but ultimately real.

The Armenians have been, since the beginning of the war, de facto belligerents, as you yourself have acknowledged, since they have fought alongside the Allies on all fronts, enduring heavy sacrifices and great suffering for the sake of their unshakeable attachment to the cause of the Entente.

The Armenian contribution to the Russian campaigns in Eastern Anatolia was also clearly displayed in New York

Times. An article entitled "Armenians Fighting Turks – Besieging Van – Others Operating in Turkish Army's Rear", published on November 7, 1914, observed that:

> A dispatch received by The Daily Telegraph from Tiflis, capital of the Government of Caucasia, by way of Moscow, says: "The Turkish town of Van (140 miles southeast of Erzerum, Turkish Armenia) is being besieged by a detachment of Armenians, who are aiding the Russians. The town has a large arsenal. Another Armenian detachment is operating in the rear of the Turkish army."

In other words, the Armenians did not just directly contribute to the Russian army but also operated to the rear of the Ottoman army to prevent it functioning properly. Small-scale rebellions began erupting in December 1914 in some districts of Van province. The Armenian rebels cut the telegraph wires (BOA. DH. ŞFR. 48/7, 2 Kanun-u evvel 1330 [15 December 1914]) and killed a number of governmental officials (BOA. DH. ŞFR. 48/182, 15 Kanun-u evvel 1330 [28 December 1914]). One month later the Zeytoun Armenians revolted, attacking gendarmes and government officials. In February 1915, an Armenian rebellion swept the entire plain of Muş (Sonyel, 2003, pp. 398-399). As the archival evidence indicates, similar small and largescale revolts occurred before the great Van rebellion stormed Eastern Anatolia. As Erickson (2011, p. 295) suggests:

> According to Ottoman intelligence reports and the reports of neutral observers, there may have been as many

as 25,000 insurgent Armenians actively conducting military operations against the empire. In fact, the cause of the insurrection was largely irrelevant since it did actualize and by the mid-spring 1915, thousands of Armenian revolutionaries were under arms and fighting under effective command and control.

The Van rebellion turned out to be the last drop that makes the glass overflow (for details, see McCarthy et.al., 2006). Accordingly, by March 1915, the Russians began to advance on Van and on 11 April 1915, the Armenian insurgents in Van began a general revolt in order to make the fall of the city to the Russians easier. As Erickson (2013, p. 161) writes:

> The uprising in the city of Van, in April 1915, was orchestrated by the Dashnaks in conjunction with a simultaneous offensive by the Russian army, which itself included Armenian legions of expatriate Ottoman citizens. It was carefully planned; the small Ottoman force in the area quickly lost control of the city, and then failed to prevent the relief of the Armenians by the advancing Russian army (Erickson, 2013, p. 161).

The rebellion in Van and the subsequent loss of the city to the Russians alarmed the Ottoman Empire. The Ottoman administration began to perceive the Armenian presence in Eastern Anatolia as a vital threat to its security. Erickson (2013, pp. 161-162, 166) interprets the Ottoman military mentality follows:

> The location of the Armenian population and areas of insurgency are critical to understanding the nature of the existential threat that it posed to the national

security of the Ottoman state. The Ottomans were fighting the Russians on the Caucasus frontier, and the British in Mesopotamia and Palestine. The lines of communications supporting those Ottoman fronts ran directly through the rear areas of the Ottoman armies in eastern Anatolia that were heavily populated by Armenian communities and, by extension, by the heavily armed Armenian revolutionary committees.

…

The Ottomans had solid evidence of large Armenian weapons caches in key city locations. There were numbers of terrorist incidents and guerrilla attacks by Armenians on Ottoman lines of communications. There were reports of Armenian desertions from the army, and thousands of armed Armenians were reported in the hills. There was an uprising in Zeitoun. An Armenian insurrection began when well-organized insurgents seized the city of Van, and Armenian regiments with the Russian Army assisted in its capture. The Allies landed at Gallipoli on 25 April and in early May the Russians began a major offensive toward Erzurum supported by Armenians. Armenian agents had come ashore numerous times on the Mediterranean coast. Lastly, the Ottomans knew that their local forces and jandarma were unable to quell the gathering insurgency.

Ultimately, the basic motive for the Armenian relocation was military security. The Armenians were perceived by the Ottoman authorities as a rebellious nationality in the context of World War I. So they should either be removed from the Russian front, while members of Armenian committees in other parts of the Ottoman Empire, whose activities were suspected of treason by the Ottoman government, were also to be relocated.

d. Other examples of relocation on the basis of military necessity:

It is evident that there was a military motive behind the Armenian relocation but was it unique? In other words, are there any examples of other forced relocations based on military motives? Historical evidence demonstrates that the Armenian relocation was not the only forced relocation in history. Relocating a group of people for security reasons or as a result of post-war resettlements has been a frequently used method in the international system. For instance, during their colonial wars with France between 1756 and 1763, the British transferred the Acadian French population from the present day Canadian coastal provinces of Nova Scotia, New Brunswick, and Prince Edward Island to the Thirteen Colonies. According to Geoffrey Plank (2003, p. 4), the aim of the British seemed to be to guarantee the security the region against the Acadian community, whom were supposed to be pro-French, and to force them to become "Protestant "faithful" subjects". Similarly, in 1830, with the Indian Removal Act adopted by the Congress, the American government forced the Cherokee, Chickasaw, Choctaw,

The Armenian relocation was not the only forced relocation in history. Relocating a group of people for security reasons or as a result of post-war resettlements has been a frequently used method in the international system.

Muscogee (Creek), and Seminole people to move from their homelands to the eastern parts of the present-day state of Oklahoma. The relocation of these peoples was carried out under extremely harsh conditions and claimed the lives of thousands of relocated Indians. Moreover, the motive behind this relocation was not military security but economic. As Ann Byers (2003, p. 4) wrote:

> Pressured by white settlers eager to occupy valuable and productive Cherokee land, the United States government began a long campaign – marked by broken treaties, false premises, racist attitudes, and threats of military force – to move the Cherokee off their territory and out of their homes and to relocate them to the "Great American Desert" west of the Mississippi River.

Another example of forced relocation is the relocation of the Ukrainians living in Poland after World War II. Accordingly, the Communist Polish government forcibly moved the Ukrainians since it perceived this community as a security threat because of the activities of the Ukrainian Insurgent Army. According to Diana Reilly (2013, p. xii), this relocation was done in order to assimilate the Ukrainian community into the general Polish population by dispersing them throughout the country.

Finally, the Japanese internment in the United States during World War II is a clear example of forced relocation. When Japan declared war on the United States and made the Pearl Harbor attack in December 1941, the Japanese living in the western coastal regions of the United States were considered to be a vital security threat for the country. It was supposed that in the event of a Japanese attack on the mainland, American citizens of Japanese ancestry might collaborate with the Japanese army against the United States. Therefore, President Roosevelt authorized the internment of the Japanese of the West coast with an Executive Order No. 9066 issued on 19 February 1942. With this executive order, local military commanders were authorized to designate military areas as "exclusion zones," from which any or all persons might be excluded. Hence thousands of Japanese American citizens were forcibly relocated in the interior of the country and settled in internment camps (Ng, 2002, pp. 13-15). When Fred Korematsu, one of these relocated Japanese American citizens, refused to obey this executive order arguing that it was unconstitutional and violated the Fifth Amendment to the United States Constitution, he was arrested and convicted. While he appealed to the Supreme Court, the latter upheld the judgment. In making the Court's decision, Judge Black argued that military security was the motive behind the executive order and not the racist prejudice against an American citizen of Japanese ancestry. He also declared that the whole Japanese-American population in the West coast had to be targeted because it was impossible to distinguish between who was loyal and who was disloyal:

> Like curfew, exclusion of those of Japanese origin was deemed necessary because of the presence of an unascertained number of disloyal members of the group, most of whom we have no doubt were loyal to this country. It was because we could not reject the finding

of the military authorities that it was impossible to bring about an immediate segregation of the disloyal from the loyal that we sustained the validity of the curfew order as applying to the whole group. In the instant case, temporary exclusion of the entire group was rested by the military on the same ground. The judgment that exclusion of the whole group was, for the same reason, a military imperative answers the contention that the exclusion was in the nature of group punishment based on antagonism to those of Japanese origin.

...

Korematsu was not excluded from the Military Area because of hostility to him or his race. He was excluded because we are at war with the Japanese Empire, because the properly constituted military authorities feared an invasion of our West Coast and felt constrained to take proper security measures, because they decided that the military urgency of the situation demanded that all citizens of Japanese ancestry be segregated from the West Coast temporarily, and, finally, because Congress, reposing its confidence in this time of war in our military leaders — as inevitably it must — determined that they should have the power to do just this. There was evidence of disloyalty on the part of some, the military authorities considered that the need for action was great, and time was short. (Korematsu v. United States, 323 U.S. 214)

As this court decision clearly indicates, even in the case of a prospective rather than an actual threat, the state could make the necessary military precautions including forced relocation. The fear of invasion and the possibility of collaboration between the Japanese Americans and the Japanese army forced the American administration to relocate the Japanese Americans. This relocation did not necessarily mean that the Japanese Americans were relocated on racial grounds but rather as the judge's opinion indicated "the need for action was great and time was short". Hence, relocation was perceived as the only possible option.

The examples of forced relocations analyzed above show that relocations may be undertaken because of military imperatives. The perception of a certain group living in a certain territory as a threat to national security might lead states to relocate them. In the Armenian case, the threat was not imaginary - it was quite real. Some Armenians did take up arms against the Ottoman Empire during World War I. They

> *Even the fear of invasion and the possibility of collaboration between the Japanese Americans and the Japanese army forced the American administration to relocate the Japanese Americans.*

collaborated with the Russian army and caused damage to Ottoman military logistics and communication lines. Of course, this never implied that the entire Armenian community constituted a vital threat to the existence of the Ottoman Empire and many innocent Armenians were forced to leave their homes. Hence, the thinking behind the Japanese American internment and the Armenian relocation was the same. However the US was more prepared and administered the relocation process more effectively. Moreover the US was not attacked by enemy troops on its own soil, it had more financial resources than the Ottoman Empire, and the Japanese Americans never resorted to armed resistance and never attempted to collaborate with the Japanese army. Therefore, the relocation of Japanese Americans was relatively easy compared to that of the Ottoman Armenians. The Armenian suffering during relocation was enormous but this suffering happened mainly because of the Ottoman inability to administer the process effectively, or to provide security for the relocated Armenians or to allocate sufficient resources for the proper organization of the relocation.

The thinking behind the Japanese American internment and the Armenian relocation was the same. However the US was more prepared and administered the relocation process more effectively.

6. The Armenian Diaspora and Armenian Relocation

The role of the Armenian Diaspora is extremely important in disseminating the Armenian genocide allegations, even exceeding the activities of the Armenian state. Indeed, the Armenian Diaspora is wealthier than the Armenians living in Armenia. Most of its members enjoy freedom of organization in their host countries and have not only established charities and solidarity movements but also political parties, pressure groups and lobbies. However, in the age of globalization, in which national consciousness is being challenged, Armenian Diaspora faces a threat from assimilation. Within this framework, Armenian genocide allegations act as a significant force for unity that reduces political differences among various Diaspora groups. Moreover, by making use of their financial assets, the Armenians of the Diaspora have also intervened in the domestic and foreign policy making processes of Armenia. This intervention creates a significant rift between the Armenian government and the Diaspora. While the Armenian governments have become aware that without normalization of relations with Turkey, it would be impossible to break the firm grip of Russia and the Armenian Diaspora on Armenian politics, most of the Diaspora groups perceive a normalization without the recognition of the "genocide" by Turkey, as a betrayal to the historical memory of the entire Armenian community.

> *Armenian genocide allegations act as a significant force for unity that reduces political differences among various Diaspora groups. Moreover, by making use of their financial assets, the Armenians of the Diaspora have also intervened in the domestic and foreign policy making processes of Armenia.*

a. Definition of the concept of "diaspora" and the Armenian Diaspora

A Diaspora can be defined as a group of "[...] people with a common origin who reside, more or less on a permanent basis, outside the borders of their ethnic or religious homeland – whether that homeland is real or symbolic, independent or under foreign control" (Shain and Barth, 2003, p. 452). In other words, Diaspora communities live outside the borders of their homeland and create a common identity based on their detachment from this homeland. According to Harris (2009, p. 147), there are several characteristics of Diaspora identity:

• The Diaspora community or its ancestors were dispersed;

• They retain a collective memory about their homeland, its history and achievements;

• They feel partly alienated in the host country;

• They regard their homeland as their ideal home to which they will someday return;

• They believe that they should collectively be committed to the safety and prosperity of their homeland;

• And they intend to continue the relationship between themselves and the homeland. The Armenian Diaspora fits into this definition.

The ancestors of the Armenian Diaspora were dispersed and they emigrated either from Anatolia or from other parts of the Middle East. They possessed a collective memory of their homeland but the negative conditions in this homeland compared to the host countries made them hesitant, if not reactant, to the idea of returning to it. In other words, Armenia was a distant idealized homeland instead of an actual ideal homeland to return to. Still, they persist in their relationship with the homeland but mostly in a somewhat arrogant manner. In other words, the Armenians of the Diaspora are criticized for their inclination to intervene in the domestic and foreign policies of the Republic of Armenia.

According to Shain and Barth (2003, pp. 463-465), the power of the Diaspora vis-à-vis the homeland is determined by several factors. First, the degree of motivation of a Diaspora community matters. The more highly motivated a Diaspora community is, the more influence it will have on the homeland's domestic and foreign policy. Secondly, the nature of the host-land is important. It determines the ability of the Diaspora to organize itself and also affects the impact of the Diaspora on the homeland. In a non-democratic host-land, development of Diaspora communities through civil society organizations would be difficult. Against this, if the host-land is a democratic country, this would contribute to the power of the Diaspora. Finally, the nature of the homeland is equally important. The weaker the homeland is, the more powerful the Diaspora will be. In all, the ideal conditions for a Diaspora to exert more influence on the homeland domestic and foreign policy are (1) a high motivation (high level of political consciousness), (2) a democratic host-land and (3) a weaker homeland (Shain and Barth, 2003, pp. 463-465). These ideal conditions seem to be present in the Armenian Diaspora. The Armenian Diaspora living in democratic countries such as the United States or France could be easily organized under efficient nongovernmental organizations or political lobbies, and could easily influence Armenian domestic and foreign policy, since the Armenian state is relatively weak compared to the host-land. Although they are the largest Armenian Diaspora, Armenians living in Russia lack effective Diaspora organizations of this kind and their level of influence over Armenia pertaining to genocide allegations is comparatively low.

b. The division and historical evolution of the Armenian Diaspora

The Armenian Diaspora is not only scattered among different countries, it is also not politically homogenous. Traditionally, the Armenians of the Diaspora were divided between three political parties established in the late nineteenth century. These are the social democratic Hinchak Party, the conservative nationalist Dashnak Party, and the liberal democratic Ramgavar

Party (Melkonian, 2011, p. 80). Each of these political organizations has their own associations and non-governmental organizations in different countries. In terms of the administration of the Diaspora community and Armenian domestic and foreign policy, these three factions have different outlooks. As Tölölyan (2000, p. 109) writes, among these different political lineages:

> [...] competition occurs at all levels: to control institutions and funds; to recruit loyal constituencies, to attract cultural producers to one vision or another of diasporic identity [...]; and to deal with the challenges produced anew at the margin, where new identities are continually elaborated as older ones are criticized or abandoned.

These differences and the fierce competition among different Diaspora communities can only be reduced by a common cause, i.e. the Armenian genocide allegations. As clearly stipulated in a report prepared by Policy Forum Armenia (PFA) (2010, p. 4) entitled "Armenia-Diaspora Relations: 20 Years since Independence":

> The Armenian Diaspora's survival and rise as a phoenix out of ashes of the Genocide as provided a strong impetus and a desire of the new generations of Armenians to succeed. The push for the international recognition of the Genocide has also helped consolidate much of the Armenian world outside of Soviet Armenia, by giving the Diaspora a meaningful, tangible unifying idea [...].

Armenian genocide allegations not only unite different factions for a single goal, namely achieving international recognition for the "Armenian genocide", but they also strengthen the Armenian identity from the threat of assimilation in the host-land. According to Alkan (2009, p. 199):

Armenians of the Diaspora place the "Armenian genocide" at the center of their discourse and continuously emphasize their victimization by the Ottoman Turks. Their main goal has been to convince the international community about the unquestionable reality of the genocide and make the international community put pressure on Turkey to force it to recognize the Armenian genocide allegations.

1915 Armenian Relocation is functioning as "chosen trauma" for the Armenians. It is an important source of weness and group identity especially for the Armenian Diasporas. This historical event occupies great place in the Armenian policies. Great part of Armenian Diaspora's activities is constituted by the struggle for the recognition of this event as "Armenian genocide".

Armenians of the Diaspora place the "Armenian genocide" at the center of their discourse and continuously emphasize their victimization by the Ottoman Turks. Their main goal has been to convince the international community about the unquestionable reality of the genocide and make the international community put pressure on Turkey to force it to recognize the Armenian genocide allegations. The activities of the Armenian Diaspora to obtain international recognition of genocide claims have evolved over time. The first post-relocation generation of Armenians in the Diaspora, who had arrived in their host-lands after the World War I, experienced a period of reconstruction. Although they had been directly exposed to the traumatic conditions of relocation, instead of focusing on their suffering, they attempted to begin a new life in a new country. As the PFA Report (2010, p. 7) indicates, "in the Diaspora, communities of Genocide survivors were in complete socio-economic and psychological disarray, having recently arrived in host countries and in desperate need of the basic structures for collective survival." Of course, suffering they had endured during the relocation was never forgotten but the Diaspora was so busy in accommodating itself to new conditions that most of its members did not voice their sufferings openly and explicitly.

This first period of reconstruction ended in 1945 with the end of World War II and the beginning of the Cold War. The consolidation of Soviet rule over Armenia produced a fierce anti-Soviet attitude in the Diaspora, particularly expressed by the Dashnaks. Accordingly, the Dashnaks did not consider Soviet Armenia to be the legitimate heir of the Armenian nation (PFA Report, 2010, p. 8). As Melkonian indicates:

> Separate existence of two segments of the Armenian people during the Cold War further increased and deepened the historical dissimilarities between the

Western and Eastern Armenians, and perpetuated among these two segments of stereotypical, mutually misinformed, and unrealistic perceptions of ethnic and political life of Armenians on the opposite side of the dividing line (quoted in Baser and Swain, 2009, p. 56)

Thus in the period between 1945 and 1965, at least some of the Diaspora groups, mainly the Dashnaks living in the Western Bloc, adopted an anti-Soviet stance. According to Dumanian (2010, p. 4), until the mid- 1960s, much of the political capital of the Armenian Diaspora was not allocated to making genocidal claims against Turkey, but against the Soviet Union.

Then the question comes: What had happened in mid-1960s resulting in the outburst then of genocidal claims by the Diaspora? The answer lays both in the transformation of the Diaspora and changing international circumstances. Until 1960s, the Armenian communities living abroad were settled properly in the host-lands. They were able to establish, direct and dominate diaspora institutions from the religious to the athletic, aesthetic and philanthropic. They prospered and preferred to use their prosperity on getting the genocide internationally recognized (Tölölyan, 2000, p. 119). Secondly, a discursive transformation was experienced; the second generation Diaspora communities, which had not directly suffered the Armenian relocation, began to define themselves not as an exiled community, but as a Diaspora. This means that, they were now fully settled in their host-lands and they had created a common identity based on the concept of Diaspora, emphasizing the bitter experiences of the past generation. In other words, the Diaspora community achieved strong political cohesion because of the Armenian genocide allegations (Tölölyan, 2000, p. 120). The post-relocation generation began to claim that the Diaspora had been experiencing the threat of "[…] assimilation and the fading memory of the genocide", described as the "white massacre" (Shain and Barth, 2003, p. 468). Hence the Diaspora directed its energy to preserve the Armenian identity into genocide discourse.

The international environment was equally available to openly express Armenian genocide allegations. Turkish-American relations began to worsen from the early 1960s onwards with the American decision to withdraw Jupiter missiles from Turkey without any prior announcement and with the Johnson Letter, in which the United States clearly warned Turkey to reverse its decision about a possible intervention in Cyprus to guarantee the security of the Turkish Cypriots. These two incidents caused Turkish-American bilateral relations to deteriorate and opened a more extensive space for the Armenian Diaspora in the United States to maneuver. Secondly, the post-Stalin Soviet Union perceived that the Armenian genocide allegations could be used against Turkey, which was a staunch NATO ally in the region. Therefore, Soviet Union first loosened its firm grip on Armenia by allowing student transfers from the Diaspora to the homeland in 1962. Armenian students from the Diaspora contributed much to the development of nationalist sentiment among their homeland counterparts (Laçiner, 2008, p. 143). Moreover, in 1964, Soviet Union established the Committee for Cultural Relations with Diaspora Armenians, whose aim was to liaise with various Armenian communities outside the Armenian homeland (PFA Report, 2010, p. 8). The Soviet Union was aware that Armenia was one of the most homogenous Soviet republics and therefore, the development of Armenian nationalism might be detrimental to the integrity of the Soviet system. So the Soviet administration channeled the energies of Armenian nationalism against Turkey (Laçiner, 2008, p. 143).

In 1965, on the 50th anniversary of the "Armenian genocide", both the Armenian Diaspora and the Armenians living in Armenia were ready to launch a full-scale campaign for genocide recognition.

All in all, in 1965, on the 50th anniversary of the "Armenian genocide", both the Armenian Diaspora and the Armenians living in Armenia were ready to launch a full-scale campaign for genocide recognition. The process started with a huge demonstration in Yerevan, permitted surprisingly by the Soviet authorities, who had never before agreed to such large-scale demonstrations. Thousands of Armenians gathered on April 24, demanding the return of their ancestral homelands and Turkish recognition of the "Armenian genocide" (Karlsson, 2007, p. 33). Similar demonstrations were held simultaneously in various countries, where the Armenian Diaspora resided. Hence 1965 was known as the *annus mirabilis* (miraculous year) for the "Armenian genocide" claims (Tölölyan, 2000, p. 121).

From 1965 to 1988, Armenian diaspora movements for genocide recognition followed two different courses. The first course consisted of political attempts to convince the international community of the existence of an "Armenian genocide". These attempts included the construction of a genocide memorial in Yerevan as a site of pilgrimage, which drew thousands of Armenians both from the homeland and the Diaspora (Adalian, 2010, p. 57).

Another method was to internationalize genocide recognition through parliamentary decisions. The first of these decisions was adopted in 1965, when the Armenian Diaspora in Uruguay were able to make the Uruguay Senate and House of Representatives to adopt a decision declaring April 24 as the "day of remembrance for the Armenian martyrs" (Lütem, 2009a, p. 89). Secondly, resolutions regarding the recognition of "Armenian genocide" were brought to the US Congress from 1975 onwards. The anti-Turkish mood in the US following the Turkish intervention in Cyprus was deftly exploited by the Armenian lobbies, which persuaded the Congress to declare April 24 as a "National Day of Remembrance of Man's Inhumanity to Man" (Laçiner, 2008, p. 190). Following this, the Southern Cypriot House of

Representatives publicly recognized the "Armenian genocide" in 1982 and linked this recognition to the Turkish intervention in Cyprus (Lütem, 2009a, p. 90). Finally, Armenian lobbies were successful in persuading the European Parliament to adopt a resolution in 1987 recognizing the "Armenian genocide". It is rather noticeable that this resolution, which is legally non-binding, was passed exactly at the time when Turkey made its application for full membership in the European Communities, although it stipulates that no legal, political or financial claims could be put forward against Turkey. The adverse reaction against this application seems to have encouraged the European Parliament to adopt this decision (Lütem, 2009a, p. 77-78).

However, not all Armenian activities were limited to the political sphere. The second course of action by the Diaspora Armenian movements was to get recognition for their genocide claims and was extremely violent. Some radical Armenians established terrorist organizations, such as ASALA (Armenian Secret Army for the Liberation of Armenia) or JCAG (Justice Commandos for the Armenian Genocide), which attacked above all Turkish diplomats and personnel serving abroad. Between 1973 and 1986, ASALA and JCAG as well as certain self-acting individuals murdered a total of 70 people, including 31 Turkish diplomats, other Turkish officials and their relatives. The terrorists also wounded 524 people, took 105 others hostage and staged 208 bombings in 20 countries, mostly in Europe (Lütem, 2009b, p. 37). These terrorist organizations not only targeted Turks, but also other citizens of European countries as well as Armenians. The terrorist activities of ASALA reached such high levels that in 1981, the secret organization carried out more international attacks (40 attacks in 11 countries) than any other terrorist organization (Jessup, 1998, p. 39). Hence these terrorist organizations took many lives while working to propagate their Armenian genocide allegations.

The second course of action by the Diaspora Armenian movements was to get recognition for their genocide claims and was extremely violent. Some radical Armenians established terrorist organizations, such as ASALA (Armenian Secret Army for the Liberation of Armenia) or JCAG (Justice Commandos for the Armenian Genocide), which attacked above all Turkish diplomats and personnel serving abroad.

Using terrorism as a means to make the international community aware of the genocide discourse proved futile. When terrorist activities turned against them, European countries placed these terrorist organizations under closer scrutiny. This forced the terrorist organizations to go underground and introduce the issue of genocide recognition into the international political scene through more parliamentary decisions and other propaganda activities including movies, concerts, exhibitions, etc. Hence, the Armenian genocide allegations turned out to be a significant theme in novels, films and other visual and audio media. They thus created a widespread artistic narrative of the 1915 incidents.

c. State-Diaspora relations in the post-Cold War period

The relationship between the Armenian Diaspora and the state of Armenia entered a new phase after the demise of the Soviet Union and the declaration of independence by the Republic of Armenia. At first the Armenian Diaspora seemed unprepared to deal with an independent homeland. For more than eighty years, they had dreamed of just such an ideal homeland; however, very few Armenians of the Diaspora believed that the USSR would collapse and an independent Armenia would emerge. As Tölölyan writes, the independence of Armenia created "a shock of statehood" (Tölölyan, 2006, p. 11). Moreover, according to Baser and Swain (2009, p. 56), "the sudden emergence of an Armenian state has created a frustration among the Diaspora with regards to the issues of "homeland" and "possible return" as well". In other words, the Armenians had long waited for a homeland but this new homeland was full of problems. It felt very puzzling for members of the Armenian Diaspora to leave their prosperous life and to return to a problematic homeland. As Tsypylma Darieva (2011, p. 3) argues, the classical form of homecoming as return migration and repatriation has lost its ability to attract second and third generation Diaspora Armenians. According to Audrey Selian (2013), there have been less than a thousand genuinely willing returnees from the West repatriated in Armenia since its independence. Instead of returning home, Armenians of the Diaspora have attempted to transform their homeland in a way attractive for themselves. Thus they have begun intervening in Armenian domestic and foreign policy making.

A second major development affecting state-Diaspora relations was the 1988 Spitak earthquake, which badly shattered Armenia's economy on the eve of independence. According to Pierre Verluise, before the earthquake, political divisions among different Diaspora communities threatened their common identity. However, he writes (1995, p. 38), the earthquake:

The Armenians had long waited for a homeland but this new homeland was full of problems. It felt very puzzling for. members of the Armenian Diaspora to leave their prosperous life and to return to a problematic homeland.

> [...] changed this situation in a single stroke by reviving the Armenian identity in the heart of the Diaspora and creating solidarity around the issue of aid to the earthquake victims. It is clear to Armenians and non-Armenians that the earthquake strengthened Armenian identity in the Diaspora as no other event could have.

The earthquake did not only unite the Armenian Diaspora, but also increased the influence of Diaspora over the Armenian state. Before 1988, the prevalent thinking in Armenia was that the state should sustain and support the Diaspora culturally (in terms of identity formation), while after 1988, these roles were reversed and the Diaspora increased its influence over the state through its financial assistance towards Armenia (PFA Report, 2010, p. 9).

Traditionally, except for the outbursts of nationalism in 1965, it was the Diaspora that felt free to practice nationalist ideologies and ideals. However, Nagorno-Karabagh crisis reversed this situation and created a significant rift between the Armenian state and the Diaspora.

Along with the 1988 earthquake and the independence of Armenia, a third significant factor affecting state-Diaspora relations was the Nagorno-Karabagh conflict. The war with Azerbaijan and the Armenian independence movement in Nagorno-Karabagh released Armenia's long suppressed ultra-nationalism. Traditionally, except for the outbursts of nationalism in 1965, it was the Diaspora that felt free to practice nationalist ideologies and ideals. However, Nagorno-Karabagh crisis reversed this situation and created a significant rift between the Armenian state and the Diaspora. Accordingly, the traditional Diaspora parties issued a communiqué in October 1988 criticizing ultra-nationalist policies in the Republic of Armenia. They argued that this war would not only use up the limited economic and human resources of a poor country, but also damage relations between Armenia and the Soviet authorities (PFA report, 2010, p. 13). This declaration was a clear disappointment for the Armenian state.

A second disappointment came with the declaration of independence. While the Armenians living in Armenia were extremely eager to declare Armenia to be an independent state, some influential Diaspora groups were more cautious. Even the Dashnaks were among these cautious groups; for them, it was not the appropriate time to declare independence (Dumanian, 2010, p. 7). Moreover, the Diaspora organizations strove hard to include a reference to the "Armenian genocide" in the declaration of independence. The Ramgavar party even went further; they were "[...] unhappy at not having a statement about Western Armenian territorial claims in the declaration" (Derderian, 2010, p. 4)

In sum, after the independence of Armenia, the relationship between the strong Armenian Diaspora and the weak Armenian state has never been smooth. Significant problems have emerged. The first of these is the lack of sufficient financial support from the Diaspora to the Armenian state. In other words, the Armenians living in Armenia accused the Diaspora of talking a lot about Armenia, but of actually contributing very little. According to Minoian and Freinkman (2007, p. 1), there has been a considerable gap between the political demands of Diaspora from the Armenian state and the modest participation of the Diaspora in Armenia's economic life. The level of Diaspora's investment and business participation has been extremely low and the Diaspora has been reluctant to contribute to the ongoing development processes in Armenia. Moreover, as the PFA Report (2010, p. 25) indicates, after an initial burst of humanitarian assistance either towards the earthquake victims or to the All-Armenian Fund, which was established for Diaspora donations for the development of Armenia, "donor fatigue" emerged. In other words, the level of economic contributions declined substantially, while the level of political intervention rose.

The Armenians living in Armenia accused the Diaspora of talking a lot about Armenia, but of actually contributing very little.

In addition to these economic considerations, the second dimension of the rift between the Diaspora and the Armenian state is the extreme penetration of Armenian politics by the Diaspora. This has been true since the outset. The first president of independent Armenia, Levon Ter-Petrossian struggled hard with the political influence of the Diaspora. Although Ter-Petrossian employed Diaspora professionals, such as Gerard Libaridian, Raffi

Hovannisian, Sebouh Tashjian and Vardan Oskanian, in his government in order to guarantee financial support from the Diaspora, he never believed very much in the Diaspora's role as a source of meaningful developmental assistance to Armenia (PFA Report, 2010, p. 18). The disagreement between the Diaspora and the government was exacerbated when the Dashnaks fiercely criticized Ter-Petrossian's policies of detachment from Russia, developing relations with Turkey, and economic privatization. In 1994 the Dashnaks were finally banned by Ter-Petrossian on charges of conspiracy, spying for Russia, terrorism, and drug smuggling. The exclusion of Dashnaks from the political scene fanned enmity between the Armenian government and the Diaspora (Derderian, 2010, p. 4).

Contrary to the Diaspora politics of Ter-Petrossian, the next president of Armenia, Robert Kocharian "[...] offered little apart from lip service in this regard but was successful in harnessing the Diaspora's political support throughout most of his tenure" (PFA Report, 2010, p. 18). He generally exploited the Diaspora's discontent with Ter-Petrossian, while he had not allowed the Diaspora to take part in the government. Moreover, when Raffi Hovannisian, Armenia's first and Us-born Foreign Minister, attempted to apply as a candidate in 2003 presidential election, his application was denied with a court decision indicating that the tenure of his Armenian citizenship was not enough for application (PFA Report, 2010, p. 18).

This cynical attitude towards the Diaspora has been largely continued by Serzh Sargsyan. However, two current problems, one domestic and the other external, damage state-Diaspora relations more. There was continuous criticism of the non-democratic policies of the regime by the Diaspora. In other words, the Diaspora based its discourse on the democratization of Armenia and perceived the current government as corrupt and consequently supported dissident movements in Armenia. The mass demonstrations in Armenia in 2008, which criticized the corruption and maladministration by the government fiercely, were clearly supported by the Armenian Diaspora (Derderian, 2010, p. 5).

The radical groups in the Armenian Diaspora have always rejected any kind of rapprochement with Turkey; they perceive such a rapprochement as a betrayal against the "reality of the Armenian genocide".

The external problem is more severe and relates to Turkish-Armenian relations. Accordingly, the radical groups in the Armenian Diaspora have always rejected any kind of rapprochement with Turkey; they perceive such a rapprochement as a betrayal against the "reality of the Armenian genocide". One of the main reasons for the forced resignation of Ter-Petrossian was his attempts to develop relations with Turkey and to end the Armenian-Azeri conflict (Shain, 2007, p. 148). Similar reactions came

95

from the Diaspora, when Turkey and Armenia decided to sign "the Protocol on Development of Relations between the Republic of Turkey and the Republic of Armenia". For example the Dashnaks protested the signature of the protocols immediately (Azatutyun, 15 September 2009). Raffi Hovannisian also rejected rapprochement of any kind with Turkey and perceived this as a betrayal of Armenian determination for internationalization of genocide recognition. He said: "There is no negotiation, there is no protocol, and there is no resolution, as important as they are, that can compensate for the depth and breadth of that transgenerational loss" (Hovannisian, 2010, p. 7). He even went further: "We cannot allow the legitimation, the legalization of our loss of homeland, of our dispossession, of our genocide, without at least simultaneously addressing the issues of history and its acknowledgment, and of education and cultural heritage, of a right of return, and of secure access to the sea" (Hovannisian, 2010, p. 9). Similarly, the French-Armenian author, Denis Donikian wrote after the signature of the protocols as follows:

> Today, this Diaspora has just received a cold shower. That is, since independence, this power for solidarity that it has represented seems to have turned to be a lost cause. By not asking for any political counterweight in exchange, the financial contributors of the Diaspora have become the cuckolds of Armenia. Not only is their assistance partially or even completely diverted [...], but it is always unilateral [...]. One is forced to admit that the Armenian Diaspora, not having a voice on the

internal political stage of the country, could not monetize its financial assistance into forcing the Armenian State to develop a real social policy. This demonstrates the level of political contempt assigned to the Diaspora Armenians which is profoundly humiliating in view of the financial interest it represents. [...] It is therefore not surprising that today the Diaspora feels cheated [...] Today, the Diaspora pays the price of having managed the suspect liabilities of the Armenian State too complacently. (Quoted in PFA Report, 2010, p. 5)

The excessive intervention of the Diaspora in Armenian politics has been criticized both within the Diaspora and by the Armenian state. Some Diaspora members themselves criticize the Diaspora for its persistence on the issues about the past and undermining the urgent needs of Armenia. As Shain mentions, "Diaspora hard liners are said to care less about the homeland's present and future than about past's dead" (quoted in Baser and Swain, p. 57). In this respect, Vahé Berberian's recent criticism of the Diaspora is quite conspicuous. As a famous Armenian artist and an eminent member of the Armenian Diaspora, Berberian (2013) clearly denounces the obsession of the Diaspora with the "Armenian genocide":

We are obsessed with the past to the point that we don't even live the present anymore [...] I can understand the obsession with Genocide on political fronts, but an obsession like that on cultural front is almost deadly, because it can create a nation of necrophiliacs: a nation that romances its dead [...O]ur cultural identity, which in my opinion, is accelerating the decline of our national identity, because there is something already dead in anything that's preserved or conserved.

Of course, this does not necessarily mean that Berberian and other Armenians of the Diaspora sharing his views deny the Armenian genocide allegations; rather they argue that the obsession with the past deprives both Armenia and the Diaspora from effective administration of the Diaspora and the homeland. Hence, without forgetting "the genocide", the Armenians should face up the contemporary political realities.

In other words, these critics emphasize that Armenia needs to ameliorate its relations with Turkey for a better future but suggest that the conservative Diaspora mentality puts an obstacle in front of it. Moreover, it is thought that the Diaspora does not really care about the homeland. As Selian (2013) writes: "At worst, we Diasporans have no clue what is going on in the nation and don't care, or we do care and continue to believe that sending a check to big philanthropic organization XYZ is going to materially, sustainably, systemically affect the life of an Armenian citizen."

In sum, at least some Armenians of the Diaspora and some political authorities in Armenia have begun to be aware of current political realities. According to them, insistence on denying any kind of negotiation with Turkey will have detrimental effects for Armenia; therefore this policy of enmity ought to be changed. For instance Richard Giragosian argues that the development of Turkish-Armenian relations will create a win-win situation.

It would enhance Turkey's record of domestic reform as well as her international position and it relieves the international pressure on Turkey for the normalization of Turkish- Armenian relations. For Armenia, the benefits of normalization are even higher. It would decrease the Armenian dependency on Russia, increase the economic well-being of the Armenians and the domestic legitimacy of the government (Giragosian, 2009, pp. 4-5). Similarly, Aras and Özbay argue that Turkey should not be obsessed with a struggle against genocide allegations and that normalization of relations would be beneficial for both states. Their (2008, pp. 5-7) policy recommendations for Turkey are as follows:

> *For Armenia, the benefits of normalization are even higher. It would decrease the Armenian dependency on Russia, increase the economic well-being of the Armenians and the domestic legitimacy of the government.*

- Turkey should treat the Armenian Diaspora and the Republic of Armenia differently, since Armenian interests differ from the Diaspora's priorities. Armenia needs to normalize relations with Turkey and so Turkey should answer this need.

- Turkey should alter its defensive stance dependent on struggling against allegations of genocide in favor of a proactive policy based on Armenian recognition of Turkey's territorial integrity and the subsequent beginning of a normalization process.

- The normalization of relations with Armenia would strengthen Turkey's regional profile in the Caucasus, and might open the way for new mediator and facilitator roles for Turkey in several Caucasian conflicts and problems. That would increase Turkey's leverage in the Nagorno-Karabagh question as well.

- Turkish moves toward normalization would generate support from the European Union, the U.S. and the international community. This support would diminish the voice of the Diaspora and contribute to the relief of Armenia from pressure from the Diaspora.

- Turkey should devote more energy to establishing a joint commission of historians to undertake an objective and scholarly study of the genocide allegations.

The Armenian Diaspora opposes this idea on the grounds that it would amount to questioning the authenticity of the genocide allegations. However, it might be easier to persuade the Armenian administration of the usefulness of such an initiative. The Armenian Diaspora insists on the Armenian genocide allegations in order to maintain its unity and sense of common identity, things threatened by political, ideological, and social differences among the

Armenians of the Diaspora and the pressures of the host cultures to assimilate them. The only way to maintain identity within the Diaspora and the political influence in the homeland as well as in the host countries is, according to the Diaspora elites, the continuation of the struggle for international recognition of the genocide allegations. However, this insistence has recently been criticized both by the Armenian government and some members of the Diaspora. The Armenian government reacts against increasing Diaspora penetration in Armenian domestic and foreign policies. It accuses the Diaspora of contributing little on Armenia while criticizing the Armenian government. Moreover, the Armenian government is increasingly aware that normalization of relations with Turkey would be beneficial for Armenia. However, the arrogant and uncompromising attitude of the Diaspora hampers it. Some members of the Diaspora also criticize the Diaspora's obsession with the past. They argue that this obsession does not contribute to the preservation of the Armenian identity, but harms its regeneration and its adaptation to current political realities. Hence, genocide allegations are on the agenda of the Diaspora not only to commemorate what happened but also for the continuation of the Diaspora's influence on Armenian politics.

7. Parliaments vs. courts: Political resolutions and legal decisions regarding the relocation of the Armenians

As mentioned in the first chapter of this study, genocide is first and foremost a crime and therefore a legal concept. According to the Genocide Convention, the only competent authority to define a particular event such as genocide is a competent tribunal of the state in the territory where the genocidal act was committed, or an international penal tribunal with jurisdiction with respect to those Contracting Parties, with its jurisdiction accepted. Without a clear decision by these legal authorities, an event can be only categorized politically as genocide, not legally, and a purely political categorization, of course, has no legal consequence.

In the case of the Armenian relocation there have been several parliamentary decisions between 1965 and the present recognizing this event as genocide. These decisions either declare that April 24 is a day of commemoration of the victims of the "Armenian genocide" (as in the case of Uruguay in 1965), or demand that Turkey restore the "inalienable rights of the Armenian people" (as in the case of Southern Cyprus in 1982), or express solidarity with the Armenian nation as victims of the "Armenian genocide" (as in the case of Lebanon in 2000) (Lütem, 2009a, pp. 89-93). Moreover, even draft resolutions threatening Turkey have been put on the agenda. In addition, there could also be attempts to penalize the denial of the so-called genocide, as it was the case in France.

Ömer Lütem (2009a, p. 88) gives a list of reasons for the adoption of parliamentary decisions of these kinds:

- The pressure from Armenian minorities or lobbies in Latin American countries such as Argentina, Chile, Uruguay, Venezuela. Then there are European and North American countries where Armenian lobbies are extremely active such as Canada, France, Italy, and Switzerland. There are also countries where Armenians constitute a significant minority such as Lebanon and Russia.

- Anti-Turkish attitudes: Greek and Southern Cypriot decisions in particular are made as a result of Turkish-Greek bilateral problems and the 1974 Turkish intervention in Cyprus to protect the Turkish Cypriots.

- Opposition to Turkish accession to the EU or anti-Turkish/anti-Muslim discourse of kind evident in the legislative organs: Belgium, France, Germany, Italy, Poland, and the Netherlands.

- The desire of certain countries, which committed either acknowledged genocide or significant crimes against humanity, to demonstrate that other states have committed these sorts of crimes as well.

These motives indicate that political, social or religious

considerations are dominant when legislative organs decide or issue statements whether 1915 relocation should be considered as genocide or not. These bodies have not acted in accordance with the Genocide Convention, nor do they have the capacity to decide on this matter; because the issue is a legal one and can only be decided by the authorities clearly stipulated in the Convention. Therefore, these decisions have no legal consequences and are solely political decisions.

a. The Court of First Instance's Judgment (2003)

Although there is no competent court ruling identifying the events of 1915 as genocide, there are many court decisions calling the "sole reality" of the Armenian genocide allegations into question. One of the most ironic court decisions in this matter came from the Court of First Instance of the European Communities (CFI). In October 2003, a group of French Armenians, Gregoire Krikorian and his wife, Suzanne Krikorian, together with an Armenian non governmental organization, Euro-Arménie ASBL, applied to the CFI arguing that they had suffered "non-material damage" with the recognition of Turkey's status as a candidate for accession to the European Union. In their view the decision contradicted the 1987 Resolution of the European Parliament, which recognized the "Armenian genocide" and claimed that Turkish non-recognition was an obstacle to full accession.

According to the Krikorians, the EP Resolution "[...] is a legal act which, in the same way as recommendations and opinions, can produce legal effects" (CFI Decision, 2003, para. 6). They further argued that this decision harmed the Armenian community; therefore they demanded a symbolic non-pecuniary damage of one euro, together with 30.000 Euros of court costs (CFI Decision, 2003, para. 1-2).

The CFI examined the application and decided on 17 December 2003 that the CFI could give a decision without hearing the observations of the defendant bodies and without opening the oral procedure, since Art. 111 of the Rules of Procedure of the CFI authorized the Court to decide, without taking further steps, when "[...] an action is manifestly lacking any foundation in law" (CFI Decision, 2003, para. 13). In other words, the CFI decided that this application had no legal basis. What is more significant is that the Court specified that the 1987 Resolution was not a legal but a political document:

> It suffices to point out that the 1987 resolution is a document containing declarations of a purely political nature, which may be amended by the Parliament at any time. It cannot therefore have binding legal consequences for its author nor, a fortiori, for the other defendant institutions (CFI Decision, 2003, para. 19).

This paragraph clearly stipulates that there is no legally binding consequence arising from the 1987 resolution of the European Parliament. It is merely a political declaration, which can be amended by the Parliament at any time. The CFI decision affirms that genocide recognition is a serious matter, which can be carried out only through competent court decisions, not through political declarations which may be abrogated or amended at any time. With this decision, the action was dismissed and the applicants had to pay the court's costs.

"It suffices to point out that the 1987 resolution is a document containing declarations of a purely political nature, which may be amended by the Parliament at any time. It cannot therefore have binding legal consequences for its author nor, a fortiori, for the other defendant institutions" CFI Decision, 2003.

b. The Judgment of Constitutional Council of France (2012)

A second court decision came from Constitutional Council of France (CC) on 28 February 2012. On 30 January 2001, the French National Assembly and Senate issued a law stating that: "France publicly recognizes the Armenian genocide of 1915" (French Law, 2001, art.1). Based on this law, the Socialist Party drafted a resolution, which recognized the denial of "Armenian genocide" as a crime punishable with imprisonment of up to one year and a fine of 45.000 Euros. This draft was adopted on 12 October 2006 by the French National Assembly with a vote of 106 in favor to 19. There were 577 members in the French National Assembly and 445 of them did not vote (Laçiner, 2008, p. 320). The French Senate rejected this draft in May 2011. Then a subsequent draft with similar content was adopted in December 2011 and in January 2012, this time the French Senate approved the draft by 127 votes to 86. However about one month after this approval, the supreme legal authority in France, the CC decided that the law recognizing the denial of "Armenian genocide" as punishable offence was contrary to the right to free speech, and so unconstitutional (CC Decision, 2012, para. 4 and art. 1). In addition, the CC noted that the law adopted in 2001 lacked any normative nature as required for a regulation to be considered to be "law", hence further questions arose about the validity of the 2001 law recognizing the "Armenian genocide".

This decision was significant in several respects. First of all it distinguished between Armenian genocide allegations and the Holocaust. It is already illegal in France to deny the Holocaust. Denial of Holocaust is a crime punishable by a year in prison and a fine of 45.000 Euros. The same punishment would have applied for the denial of Armenian genocide allegations, if the bill had passed. Those supporting the bill tried to equate the Holocaust and the Armenian genocide allegations. For instance, Senator Hervé Marseille, one of the bill's supporters, argued that since France already recognizes the Ottoman-era killings as genocide, the same standard that applies to Holocaust denial should apply to the Armenian case (CNN, 28 February 2012). The CC, on the contrary, clearly distinguished between these two. Although Holocaust denial is a crime punishable by law, challenging the Armenian genocide allegations is considered within the context of free speech, despite the fact that France had already recognized 1915 events as genocide. This indicates that the French legal mechanism was aware of the political nature of this law and was able to rule on the unconstitutionality of the bill given the recognition of genocide allegations. Those opposed to the bill argued that genocide is a sensitive concept and it should not be trivialized so easily. According to Senator Jacques Mezard, an opponent of the legislation, such contested issues should be left to historical and academic research; otherwise the definition of genocide could be enlarged in a way to mislabel every massacre as genocide (CNN, 28 February 2012).

According to Senator Jacques Mezard, an opponent of the legislation, such contested issues should be left to historical and academic research; otherwise the definition of genocide could be enlarged in a way to mislabel every massacre as genocide.

c. The European Court of Human Rights Judgment (2013)

Although the political nature of parliamentary decisions and their legal invalidity has been affirmed directly (as with the CFI decision) or indirectly (as in the case of the CC decision) by court decisions, these courts did not openly question the validity of Armenian genocide allegations. While the CFI ruled that the application by Krikorians was procedurally invalid, the CC preferred to approach the issue in terms of the right to free speech. A third and recent court decision by the European Court of Human Rights (ECHR) directly questions the representation of Armenian genocide allegations as the sole truth, although, similar to CC, its basic concern is the violation of the the right to free speech. The case started with an application by Doğu Perinçek, the Chairman of the Turkish Worker's Party, to the ECHR. In various lectures given in Switzerland by Perinçek, he described the "Armenian genocide" as an "international lie". As a result, the "Switzerland-Armenia" Association filed a criminal complaint against him on 15 July 2005 and, on 9 March 2007, the Lausanne Police Court found him guilty of racial discrimination and argued that his motives "[…] were of racist tendency and did not contribute to the historical debate" (ECHR Press Release, 17 December 2013, pp.1-2).

Following this decision, Perinçek applied to the Criminal Cassation Division of the Vaud Cantonal Court but the

Court dismissed his application arguing that "[...] the Armenian genocide, like the Jewish genocide, was a proven historical fact, recognized by the Swiss legislature on the date of the adoption of Article 261bis of the Criminal Code" (ECHR Press Release, 17 December 2013, p. 2). A further appeal to the Federal Court was dismissed as well on 12 December 2007. Finally, having exhausted all domestic legal avenues, Perinçek decided to apply to the ECHR on the basis that his right to free speech had been violated by the Swiss courts. The court ruled in the case Perinçek v. Switzerland that Perinçek's right to free speech had been violated. This was the decision of the ECHR; however, beyond that, the text of the decision was revolutionary in the sense that it also clearly drew into question perceptions of Armenian genocide allegations as a fundamental reality.

First of all, the decision repeated that "[...] the free exercise of the right to openly discuss questions of a sensitive and controversial nature was one of the fundamental aspects of freedom of expression and distinguished a tolerant and pluralistic democratic society from a totalitarian or dictatorial regime" (ECHR Decision, 2013, para. 52). In other words, making the discussion of controversial and sensitive issues impossible by punishing debating on them without any elements of incitement to hatred or racial discrimination would be against the right to free speech, a basic human right. This implies that the Armenian genocide allegations constitute a controversial and as yet unproven issue. Any attempt to prevent sound discussion on this issue shall be considered as a violation of human rights. This general view of the ECHR implies that the activities of the Armenian Diaspora as well as those of the Armenian state which present the 1915 relocation as genocide in a way that prevents and condemns the expression of alternative narratives constitute a clear violation of the right to free speech.

Secondly, the ECHR decision indicates that the "Armenian genocide" is not an unquestionable historical fact. First of all, the ECHR stresses that genocide is a legal concept and one, which is precisely defined. According to the existing definition, it underlines that the legal definition of genocide is quite restricted and it is very difficult to prove that a crime constitutes a genocide. On the other hand, the ECHR emphasizes that there is no general consensus on the definition of 1915 events and to substantiate its claim, the ECHR argues that only about 20 states out of 190 have recognized the Armenian "genocide". (ECHR Press Release, 17 December 2013, p. 3).

It is implied that the Armenian genocide allegations pose a controversial and as yet an unproven issue. Any attempt to prevent sound discussion on this issue shall be considered as a violation of human rights.

Third, the ECHR decision clearly distinguishes between the Holocaust and the Armenian genocide allegations.

People who regard the 1915 relocation as genocide generally label this relocation as "the first Holocaust" (Fisk, 2007) and so its denial should be punished exactly as the denial of Holocaust is punished in Europe. However, the ECHR decision argues that the applications of Holocaust-deniers to the ECHR have been dismissed because the genocidal nature of the Holocaust is legally proven

The ECHR emphasizes that there is no general consensus on the definition of 1915 events and to substantiate its claim, the ECHR argues that only about 20 states out of 190 have recognized the Armenian "genocide".

and there is a clear legal basis of this incident determined by a competent international court (i.e., the Nuremberg Trials) (ECHR Press Release, 17 December 2013, p. 4). This emphasis on the legal basis of Holocaust implies that such a concrete legal basis is lacking in the Armenian relocation case.

In short the ECHR does not deem necessary to reach a conclusion concerning Armenian genocide allegations but rather it argues that

The ECHR decision clearly distinguishes between the Holocaust and the Armenian genocide allegations.

denying 1915 relocation as genocide is just as valid as accepting it as genocide. In other words, it draws attention to the disputable nature of the genocide claims. However, it implies that the Armenian genocide allegations cannot be substantiated as clearly as the Holocaust and therefore accepting the "Armenian genocide" as a fact and doing so in a way which hampers sound discussion on this controversial issue would be contrary to the right to free speech. Moreover, the accusation of "denialism", made by persons who accept the Armenian genocide allegations against those people reject the validity of the allegations, is dismissed by this decision. For denialism, there must be a real genocide, one proved and established in law but, in the Armenian case, this fundamental aspect is lacking.[1]

Conclusion

Turks and Armenians have extensive mutual historical memories. For centuries, they lived together, sharing each other's happiness as well as their sorrows. They sometimes clashed and sometimes acted together against common enemies. Armenians lived and prospered under the Ottoman Empire. They benefitted from the successes and economic accomplishments of the Empire but they also experienced bitter conditions, when the Empire was in decline. In other words, the fates of the Turks and Armenians were intertwined. However, towards the late nineteenth century, a group of Armenians began to perceive the disintegration of the Empire as an

---

1   The Swiss government has appealed for a review of the ECHR decision of 17 December 2013.

opportunity to declare their independence. They were supported by some of the Great Powers of the time not for their own sake but because of the interests of these powers. They were not aware that the decline of the Ottoman Empire would also mean the decline of the wealth and prosperity of the Armenian community as well. Hence, this politicized group of Armenians began dominating the entire Armenian community with the aim of inciting them to rise against the Ottoman Empire.

The Armenian community was right in protesting against deteriorating economic and political conditions of the Ottoman Empire. However, they were unaware of the fact that not only themselves, but the other communities of the Ottoman Empire, including the dominant Turkish community had also been experiencing similar negative conditions. Moreover, the politicized elite of the Armenian community pressed harder for independence, particularly after their disillusionment about the restoration of the Ottoman constitution as it failed to improve the deterioration. Meanwhile the Ottoman administration encountered its worst trauma with the Balkan Wars. Almost the entire European territory of the Empire were occupied and a massive wave of migration by the Balkan Muslims shook the very foundations of the imperial psyche. The Ottoman administration viewed this tragedy as treason by the former subjects of the Empire (i.e., the newly established Balkan states). Hence the continuation of Armenian political agitation for independence created significant disillusionment for the Ottoman administration as well.

In this environment of mutual distrust, World War I erupted. The Ottoman administration expected the Armenians not to ally with their adversaries; indeed some loyal Armenians continued to be employed in the Ottoman bureaucracy contributing to the Ottoman efforts to defend the territorial integrity of the Empire. Others however clearly collaborated with the enemies of the Empire. They fought against the Ottomans in Russian, and later French, armies. They organized sabotage activities to cut the logistical and communication lines of the Ottoman army. They provided intelligence for the adversaries of the Empire, and they initiated significant revolts against the Ottoman administration to help the enemy troops advance further. The Ottoman government then, decided to put a stop to this vital threat and to relocate the Armenians. This relocation was a disaster. Although the government attempted to take necessary precautions for the security of the relocated Armenians, both financial and military resources were inadequate. In

The Armenian relocation was a disaster. Although the government attempted to take necessary precautions for the security of the relocated Armenians, both financial and military resources were inadequate.

most of the cases, the government failed to administer the relocation process properly; thousands of Armenians lost their lives on the way of relocation because of lack of enough alimentation, widespread epidemics, attacks of irregular local bands and sometimes ill-treatment by some individual Ottoman officials. This was a tragedy for the Ottoman Armenians.

Acknowledging the Armenian sufferings during the process of relocation is a humanitarian issue. Everyone should be aware of the tragedy that they experienced during World War I. However Armenian suffering should not be isolated from the suffering of other communities of the Empire. It was not only the Armenians who were displaced during the turbulent second decade of the twentieth century. Thousands of Greeks, Turks, Kurds, or Arabs had been forced to leave their homes, villages and towns. It was not only the Armenians who had suffered in the hands of the Turks and the Kurds during World War I; thousands of Turks and Kurds were massacred by the Armenians as well. Not only had the Armenians experienced desolation and grief; the entire communities of the Empire suffered tremendously. In other words, the tragedy was common to all sides and hence that tragedy has to be explored in its totality, not by isolating the suffering of one community in a way to neglect the suffering of the others.

Indeed what Turkey has offered for almost a decade, is to to achieve a "just memory" which recpect the sufferings of all. In 2005, Turkey offered to establish a commission of joint historians, including not only Turkish and Armenian historians, but also historians from all over the world, who are eager to contribute to reveal the historical reality. This offer was rejected by the Armenian side on the grounds that it would downgrade the status of the 1915 relocation from that of genocide to something else. The Armenian Diaspora in particular, influenced the government of Armenia not to abandon backing efforts at obtaining international recognition of the Armenian genocide allegations. This pressure on the government was required not only for international recognition of genocide claims, but also for strengthening the diasporic identity. The Diaspora is so divided politically that the one thing which unites its fragments has always been the genocide allegations. To this end the Diaspora has not hesitated to brand the 1915 relocation as the "first Holocaust" of the modern era.

But is it so? Could the Ottoman treatment of Armenians be compared with the Nazi treatment of the Jews?

When the historical evolution of two cases is taken into consideration significant differences appear. The Jews did not revolt against the German state but the Armenians did so against the Ottoman Empire. The Jews never established political organizations for an independent Jewish political entity in Germany but Armenian political organizations aimed at independence from the very beginning. The Jews did not support enemy troops or deprive the German army from proper logistics and communications, but Armenian volunteers fought in the Russian army against the Ottoman Empire and obstructed proper logistics for the Ottoman army during its war against the Russian army. Moreover, there was no Jewish rebellion, say in Leipzig, to assist the Russian invasion of the city. However, the Armenian guerillas did initiate a fierce rebellion in Van, resulting in the occupation of the city by Russian troops. The Jews of Berlin were not immune from persecution nor were their religious leaders but the Armenians of Istanbul (except for those convicted of political activities against the state) together with their Patriarch were immune from relocation. There were no Jewish civil servants serving in German civil service under the Nazi regime whereas the CUP administration did not hesitate to employ Armenians in Ottoman civil service. Jews were exterminated by the Nazi regime just for being Jews but there was no systematic racial hatred of that kind against the Armenians even during the process of relocation.

Questioning the validity of the Armenian genocide

allegations does not imply any denial of the suffering of Armenians during the relocation. Questioning the allegations is simply intended to counter possible prejudicial and unfair treatment of the Turkish narrative. The Armenian relocation was a historical event, whereas the crime of genocide is a matter of law. Hence history and law, not politics, are the disciplines that should be employed to study the Armenian relocation and genocide allegations. As regards historical analysis, Turkish governments continually reiterate their offer to establish a joint historians' commission. Such a commission would work independently and whole archives would be opened to facilitate its studies. As regards law, there has been no competent court decision defining the 1915 relocation as genocide, so under the Genocide Convention, it is impossible to define this incident legally as genocide. The ECHR's recent decision shows that there is no consensus about the definition of the 1915 relocation as genocide: only 20 states out of 190 have recognized the genocide allegations. Moreover, the CFI clearly stated in 2003 that parliamentary resolutions are political not legal acts, which can be amended or abrogated at any time. Hence, they do not create legal consequences.

> *Questioning the validity of the Armenian genocide allegations never means the denial of the suffering of Armenians during the relocation.*

All in all, the 1915 relocation and the common tragedy

experienced during World War by the Muslim and Armenian populations of the Ottoman Empire should be studied without politicization or prejudice. In other words, these topics should not be made part of the political structure and abused for daily political purposes. Rather, they should be investigated with academic dignity and objectivity. In the same context, relations between Turkey and Armenia should also be freed from the chains of the past. Current political issues, including opening the Turkish-Armenian border, the Nagorno-Karabakh problem, and the Armenian nonrecognition of Turkey's territorial integrity have already occupied the agenda of these two states. Instead of focusing on the tragedies of the past and consuming their time and energy on fruitless debates about genocide recognition and denial, the policy-makers of the two states should take incremental but stable steps to normalize their bilateral relations. Leaving the debates of 1915 relocation to historians would never imply forgetting this tragedy. It is rather that depoliticizing these debates would contribute to the enhancement of mutual understanding, something which would open the way for the normalization of Turkish-Armenian relations.

Bibliography
A. Newspaper Articles and Legal Documents

1. Meclis-i Mebusan Zabıt Ceridesi (MMZC), Vol. 1, Session 1, 1 Mayıs 1330 [14 May 1914], URL: http://www.tbmm.gov.tr/tutanaklar/ TUTANAK/MECMEB/mmbd03-ic01c001/mmbd03ic01 c001ink001.pdf (Accessed on 22.04.2014).

2. "Dashnaks Stage More Protests against Turkey-Armenia Deal", Azatutyun, 15 September 2009. URL: http://www.azatutyun.am/content/article/1823228. html (Accessed on 22.04.2014).

3. "French Senate passes Armenian genocide law", BBC News, 23 January 2012. URL: http://www.bbc.co.uk/news/world-europe-16677986 (Accessed on 22.04.2014).

4. "French court overturns Armenian genocide denial law", CNN, 28 February 2012. URL: http://edition.cnn.com/2012/02/28/world/europe/france-armenia-genocide/index.html (Accessed on 22.04.2014).

5. "Armenians Fighting Turks – Besieging Van – Others Operating in Turkish Army's Rear", New York Times, 7 November 1914, taken from URL:http://query.nytimes.com/gst/abstract.html?res=F60B1EFF3C5C13738 DDDAE0894-D9415B848DF1D3 (Accessed on 22.04.2014).

6. "Criminal conviction for denial that the atrocities perpetrated against the Armenian people in 1915 and years after constituted genocide was unjustified", ECHR Press Release, 17 December 2013 https://www.google.com.tr/url?sa=t&rct=j&q=&esrc=s&source=web&cd =1&ved=0CC4QFjAA&url=http%3A%2F%2Fhud oc.echr.coe.int%2Fwebservices%2Fcontent%2Fpdf%

2F003-4613832-5581451&ei=tar4Up2pOciI0AW0pI
G4BQ&usg=AFQjCNGrVI2QmuCFhUm8tI8kovA-
R8jkKg& sig2=_no1iLhTnEw0TpcWaVcXNw&bvm=
bv.60983673,d.d2k&cad=rjt (Accessed on 22.04.2014).

7. European Parliament, "Resolution on a Political Solution
to the Armenian Question", Doc. A2-33/87, 18 June
1987. URL: http://www.europarl.europa.eu/intcoop/
euro/pcc/aag/pcc_meeting/resolutions/ 1987_07_20.pdf
(Accessed on 22.04.2014).

8. Court of First Instance of the European Communities,
Krikorian and Oth ers v. Parliament and Others, Case
T-346/03, 17 December 2003. URL: http://curia.
europa.eu/juris/showPdf.jsf;jsessionid=9ea7d2dc30d
b34e25f0 e6db74be187eabef9520c3498.e34KaxiLc3
qMb40Rch0SaxuMbNb0?text =&docid=48869&pa
geIndex=0&doclang=en&mode=lst&dir=&occ=first
&part=1&cid=142048 (Accessed on 22.04.2014).

9. "Loi n° 2001-70 du 29 janvier 2001 relative à la
reconnaissance du génocide arménien de 1915". URL:
http://legifrance.gouv.fr/affichTexte. do?cidTexte=
JORFTEXT000000403928 (22.04.2014).

10. ECHR Decision, *Affaire Perinçek c. Suisse*, No. 27510/08,
17 December 2013, URL: http://hudoc.echr.coe.int/
sites/eng/Pages/search.aspx#{"fulltext": ["perinçek"]," do
cumentcollectionid2":["GRANDCHAMBER","CHAM
BER"]} (Accessed on 22.04.2014).

11. Constitutional Council of France, "Law on the
punishment of denials of the existence of genocides
recognised by law", No. 2012-647 DC, 29 February
2012. URL: http://www.conseil-constitutionnel.fr/
conseil-constitutionnel/english/caselaw/ decision/
decision-no-2012-647-dc-of-28-february-2012.114637.
html (Accessed on 22.04.2014).

B. Books and Articles

1. Kamel S. Abu Jaber, "The Millet System in The Nineteenth-Century Ottoman Empire, *The Muslim World*, Vol. 57, No. 3, July 1967, pp. 212– 223.

2. Rouben Paul Adalian, *Historical Dictionary of Armenia*, 2nd ed., Lanham, MD: Scarecrow Press, 2010.

3. Taner Akçam, *İnsan Hakları ve Ermeni Sorunu, İttihat Terakki'den Kurtuluş Savaşı'na*, 2nd ed., Ankara: İmge Kitabevi, 2002.

4. Taner Akçam, *From Empire to Republic: Turkish Nationalism and the Armenian Genocide*, London and New York, NY: Zed Books, 2004.

5. Taner Akçam ve Ümit Kurt, *Kanunların Ruhu: Emval-i Metruke Kanunlarında Soykırımın İzini Sürmek*, İstanbul: İletişim Yayınları, 2012.

6. Gündüz Aktan, "The Armenian Problem and International Law", in Ömer Engin Lütem (ed.), *The Armenian Question: Basic Knowledge and Documentation*, Ankara: Terazi Publishing, 2009, pp. 131-169.

7. Sevinç Göral Alkan, "The Turkish-Armenian Issue from the Perspective of Psychology and Psychoanalysis: Victimization and Large Group Identity", ", in Ömer Engin Lütem (ed.), *The Armenian Question: Basic Knowledge and Documentation*, Ankara: Terazi Publishing, 2009, pp. 191- 202.

8. Aram Andonian, *Documents Officiels Concernant les Massacres Arméniens*, Paris: Imprimerie H. Turabian, 1920.

9. Bülent Aras and Fatih Özbay, "Turkish-Armenian Relations: Will Football Diplomacy Work?", *SETA Policy Brief*, No. 24, 2008, pp. 1-7.

10. Feridun Ata, "Divân-ı Harb-i Örfî Mahkemelerinde Ermeni Tehciri Yargılamaları", *Türkiyat Araştırmaları Dergisi*, No. 14, Autumn 2004, pp. 297-323.

11. Feridun Ata, *İşgal İstanbul'unda Tehcir Yargılamaları*, Ankara: Türk Tarih Kurumu Yayınları, 2005.

12. Howard Ball, *Genocide: A Reference Handbook*, Santa Barbara, CA: ABC Clio, 2011.

13. Bahar Baser and Ashok Swain, "Diaspora Design versus Homeland Realities: Case Study of Armenian Diaspora", *Caucasian Review of International Affairs*, Vol. 3, No. 1, 2009, pp. 45-62.

14. Vahé Berberian, "The Armenian Condition in the Diaspora", California Courier Online, 29 December 2013.

15. Niyazi Berkes, *Development of Secularism in Turkey*, 2nd ed., London: Hurst&Company, 1998.

16. Maurits H. van den Boogert, "Millets: Past and Present", in Anne Sofie Roald and Anh Nga Longva (eds.), *Religious Minorities in the Middle East: Domination, Self-Empowerment, Accommodation*, Leiden: Brill, 2011, pp. 27-46.

17. George A. Bournoutian, *A Concise History of the Armenian People: From Ancient Times to the Present*, Costa Mesa, CA: Mazda Publishers, 2002.

18. Ann Byers, *The Trail of Tears: A Primary Source History of the Forced Relocation of the Cherokee Nation*, New York, NY: The Rosen Publishing Group, 2003.

19. Frank Chalk, "Redefining Genocide", in George J. Andreopoulos (ed.), *Genocide: Conceptual and Historical Dimensions, Philadelphia*, PA: University of Pennsylvania Press, 1997, pp. 47-63.

20. Tim Chapman, *The Congress of Vienna: Origins, Processes, and Results*, London and New York, NY: Routledge, 1998.

21. Richard Clogg, *A Concise History of Greece*, 3rd ed., Cambridge: Cambridge University Press, 2013.

22. Gomidas Çarkçıyan, *Türk Devleti Hizmetinde Ermeniler*, İstanbul: Kesit Yayınları, 2006.

23. Kemal Çiçek, *Ermenilerin Zorunlu Göçü* (1915-1917), Ankara: Türk Tarih Kurumu Yayınları, 2005.

24. Vahakn Dadrian, *The History of the Armenian Genocide: Ethnic Conflict from the Balkans to Anatolia to the Caucasus*, Oxford and New York: Berghahn Books, 2004a.

25. Vahakn Dadrian, *Warrant for Genocide: Key Elements of Turco-Armenian Conflict*, 2nd ed., New Brunswick, NJ: Transaction Publishers, 2004b.

26. Vahakn Dadrian and Taner Akçam, *Judgment at Istanbul: The Armenian Genocide Trials*, Oxford and New York, NY: Berghahn Books, 2011.

27. Tsypylma Darieva, "Come to Move Mountains: Diaspora and Development in a Transnational Age", *Caucasus Analytical Digest*, No. 29, 2011, pp. 2-4.

28. Dzovinar Derderian, "Democracy in Armenia and Diaspora-Armenia Relations", Paper presented to *the Second Annual PFA Forum on Armenia- Diaspora Relations*, February 28 – March 2, 2010, Washington D.C. Taken from the URL: http://www.pf-armenia.org/sites/default/files/uploads/ pfa_uploads/Diaspora_Forum/Derderian-Democracy_Armenia.pdf.

29. Henry Dumanian, "Diaspora and Democracy: The Diaspora's Response to National Movements in Armenia", Paper presented to *the Second Annual PFA Forum on Armenia-Diaspora Relations*, February 28 – March 2, 2010, Washington D.C. Taken from the URL:

http://www.pfarmenia. org/sites/default/files/uploads/ pfa_uploads/ Diaspora_Forum/Dumanian- PFA_ forum_paper.pdf.

30. Fuat Dündar, *Crime of Numbers: The Role of Statistics in the Armenian Question (1878-1918)*, Westport, CT: Greenwood Publishing Group, 2010.

31. Edward J. Erickson, "The Armenians and Ottoman Military Policy, 1915", *War in History*, Vol 15, No. 2, 2008, pp. 141-167.

32. Edward J. Erickson, "The Armenian Relocations and Ottoman National Security: Military Necessity or Excuse for Genocide?", *Middle East Critique*, Vol. 20, No. 3, 2011, pp. 291-298.

33. Edward J. Erickson, *Ottomans and Armenians: A Study in Counterinsurgency*, New York, NY: Palgrave Macmillan, 2013.

34. Erich Feigl, *A Myth of Terror – Armenian Extremism: Its Causes and Its Historical Context*, Salzburg: Edition Zeitgeschichte,1986.

35. Carter Vaughn Findley, *Bureaucratic Reform in the Ottoman Empire: The Sublime Porte*, 1789-1922, Princeton, NJ: Princeton University Press, 1980.

36. Robert Fisk, "The Forgotten Holocaust", *Independent*, 28 August 2007. Taken from URL: http://www. independent.co.uk/voices/commentators/fisk/robert-fisk-theforgotten- holocaust-463306.html.

37. Caroline Fournet, *The Crime of Destruction and the Law of Genocide: Their Impact on Collective Memory*, London: Ashgate Publishing, 2007.

38. David Gaunt, *Massacres, Resistance, Protectors: Muslim-Christian Relations in Eastern Anatolia during World War I*, Piscataway, NJ: Gorgias Press LLC, 2006.

39. Maxime Gauin, "Aram Andonian's Memoirs of Naim Bey and the Contemporary Attempts to Defend Their 'Authenticity'", *Review of Armenian Studies*, No. 23, 2011, pp. 233-292.

40. Richard Giragosian, "Changing Armenia-Turkish Relations", *Fokus Südkaukasus*, 2009. Taken from URL: http://library.fes.de/pdf-files/bueros/georgien/06380.pdf.

41. Erika Harris, *Nationalism: Theories and Cases*, Edinburgh: Edinburgh University Press, 2009.

42. Kevin Jon Heller, *The Nuremberg Military Tribunals and the Origins of International Criminal Law*, Oxford: Oxford University Press, 2011.

43. Metin Heper and Nur Bilge Criss, *Historical Dictionary of Turkey*, 3rd ed., Lanham, MD: Scarecrow Press, 2009.

44. Richard Hovannisian (ed.), *The Armenian Genocide in Perspective*, "10th ed., New Brunswick, NJ: Transaction Publishers, 2007.

45. Raffi K. Hovannisian, "Keynote Address", Paper presented to *the Second Annual PFA Forum on Armenia-Diaspora Relations*, February 28 – March 2, 2010, Washington D.C. Taken from the URL: http://www.pf-armenia.org/sites/default/files/uploads/ pfa_uploads/ Diaspora_ Forum/Raffi_H_PFA_Forum.pdf.

46. John E. Jessup, *An Encyclopedic Dictionary of Conflict and Conflict Resolution, 1945-1996*, Westport, CT: Greenwood Publishing Group, 1998.

47. Klas-Göran Karlsson, "Memory of Mass Murder. The Genocide in Armenian and non-Armenian Historical Consciousness", in Conny Mithander, John Sundholm, Maria Holmgren Troy (eds.), *Collective Traumas:*

Memories of War and Conflict in 20ᵗʰ-Century Europe, Brussels: Peter Lang, 2007, pp. 13-46.

48. Efraim Karsh and Inari Karsh, *Empires of the Sand: The Struggle for Mastery in the Middle East, 1789-1923*, Cambridge, MA: Harvard University Press, 2001.

49. Hovannes Katchznouni, *The Armenian Revolutionary Federation (Dashnagtzoutiun) Has Nothing to Do Any More*, New York, NY: Armenian Information Service, 1955.

50. Charles King, *The Ghost of Freedom: A History of the Caucasus: A History of the Caucasus*, Oxford: Oxford University Press, 2008.

51. Guenter Lewy, *The Armenian Massacres in Ottoman Turkey: A Disputed Genocide*, Salt Lake City, UT: The University of Utah Press, 2005.

52. Guenter Lewy, "Revisiting the Armenian Genocide," *Middle East Quarterly*, Vol 7, No. 4, Fall 2005, pp. 3-12.

53. Gerard Libaridian, *Modern Armenia: People, Nation, State*, 2ⁿᵈ ed., New Brunswick, NJ: Transaction Publishers, 2004.

54. Ömer Engin Lütem, "The Armenian Question Today", in Ömer Engin Lütem (ed.), *The Armenian Question: Basic Knowledge and Documentation*, Ankara: Terazi Publishing, 2009a, pp.77-120.

55. Ömer Engin Lütem, "The Armenian Question from Lausanne to the Present", in Ömer Engin Lütem (ed.), *The Armenian Question: Basic Knowledge and Documentation*, Ankara: Terazi Publishing, 2009b, pp. 29-42.

56. Andrew Mango, "Atatürk", in Reşat Kasaba (ed.), *Cambridge History of Modern Turkey, Volume 4: Turkey in the Modern World*, Cambridge: Cambridge University Press, 2006, pp. 147-172.

57. Justin McCarthy, Esat Arslan, Cemalettin Taşkıran and Ömer Turan, *The Armenian Rebellion at Van*, Salt Lake City, UT, University of Utah Press, 2006.

58. Eduard Melkonian, "Imported Politics: Diaspora Political Parties in Armenia's Domestic Landscape", in Alexander Iskandaryan (ed.), *Identities, Ideologies and Institutions: A Decade of Insight into the Caucasus – 2001- 2011*, Yerevan: Caucasus Institute, 2011, pp. 79-88.

59. Robert Melson, *Revolution and Genocide: On the Origins of the Armenian Genocide and the Holocaust*, Chicago, IL: University of Chicago Press, 1996.

60. Victoria Minoian and Lev Freinkman, "Diaspora's Contribution to Armenia's Economic Development: What Drives the First Movers and How Their Efforts Could Be Scaled Up?", *World Bank Working Paper*, No. 39381, 2007, pp. 1-21.

    http://www-wds.worldbank.org/external/default/ WDSContentServer/ WDSP/IB/ 2007/04/10/ 000090341_20070410160519/Rendered/PDF/ 393810AM0Diasporas0 contribution01PUBLIC1.pdf

61. Louise Nalbandian, *The Armenian Revolutionary Movement: The Development of Armenian Political Parties through the Nineteenth Century*, Berkeley, Los Angeles, CA: University of California Press, 1963.

62. Wendy L. Ng, *Japanese American Internment during World War II: A History and Reference Guide*, Westport, CT: Greenwood Publishing Group, 2002.

63. Efthymios Nicolaidis, *Science and Eastern Orthodoxy: From the Greek Fathers to the Age of Globalization*, Baltimore, MD: Johns Hopkins University Press, 2011.

64. Şinasi Orel and Süreyya Yuca, The Talât Pasha 'Telegrams':

Historical Fact or Armenian Fiction?, Nicosia: K. Rustem and Brother, 1986.

65. Ergun Özbudun, "Turkey", in Myron Weiner and Ergun Özbudun (eds.), *Competitive Elections in Developing Countries*, Durham, NC: Duke University Press, 1987.

66. Melek Öksüz, "Amerikan Belgelerine Göre I. Dünya Savaşı ve Mütareke Dönemlerinde Osmanlı Hükümetleri", *Turkish Studies*, Vol. 5, No. 1, 2010, pp. 1247-1270.

67. Razmik Panossian, "The Past as Nation: Three Dimensions of Armenian Identity", *Geopolitics*, Vol. 7, No. 2, 2002, pp. 121-146.

68. Kapriel Serope Papazian, *Patriotism Perverted: A Discussion of the Deeds and the Misdeeds of the Armenian Revolutionary Federation, the So- Called Dashnagtzoutune*, Watertown, MA: Baikar Press, 1934.

69. Geoffrey Gilbert Plank, *An Unsettled Conquest: The British Campaign Against the Peoples of Acadia*, Philadelphia, PA: University of Pennsylvania Press, 2003.

70. John B. Quigley, *The Genocide Convention: An International Law Analysis*, London: Ashgate Publishing, Ltd., 2006.

71. Shirley Elson Roessler and Reny Miklos, *Europe 1715- 1919: From Enlightenment to World War*, Oxford: Rowman & Littlefield Publishers, 2003.

72. Policy Forum Armenia, "Armenia-Diaspora Relations, 20 Years since Independence", 2010, taken from URL: http://www.pf-armenia.org/sites/default/files/documents/files/PFA%20Diaspora%20Report.pdf (Last Access: 07.08.2014).

73. Diana Howansky Reilly, *Scattered: The Forced Relocation of Poland's Ukrainians after World War II*, Madison, WI: University of Wisconsin Press, 2013.

74. Jeremy Salt, *Imperialism, Evangelism and the Ottoman Armenians, 1878- 1896*, 2nd ed., London: Routledge, 2013.

75. Jeremy Salt, *The Unmaking of the Middle East: A History of Western Disorder in Arab Lands*, Berkeley, CA: University of California Press, 2008.

76. Yusuf Sarınay, "What Happened on April 24, 1915?, A Case Study on the Circular of 24 April 1915 and Arrest of the Armenian Committee Members in Istanbul", *International Journal of Turkish Studies*, Vol. 14, No. 1-2, 2008, pp. 75-101.

77. Yusuf Sarınay, *24 Nisan 1915'te Ne Oldu? Ermeni Sevk ve İskanının Perde Arkası*, İstanbul: İdeal Yayıncılık, 2012.

78. William A. Schabas, *Genocide in International Law: The Crime of Crimes*, 2nd ed., Cambridge: Cambridge University Press, 2009.

79. Audrey Selian, "All Is Not Well in Diaspora-Homeland Relations: The Diasporan Perspective", Taken from the URL:http://www.armenianweekly.com/2013/10/18/all-is-not-well-in-Diaspora-homeland-relationsthe-Diasporan-perspective/.

80. Yossi Shain and Aharon Barth, "Diasporas and International Relations Theory" *International Organization*, Vol. 57, No. 3, 2003, pp. 449-479.

81. Yossi Shain, *Kinship & Diasporas in International Affairs*, Ann Arbor, MI: University of Michigan Press, 2007.

82. Thomas W. Simon, *The Laws of Genocide: Prescriptions for a Just World*, Westport, CT: Greenwood Publishing Group, 2007.

83. Salahi R. Sonyel, *Minorities and the Destruction of the Ottoman Empire*, Ankara: Turkish Historical Society Printing House, 1993.

84. Philip Stoddard, *The Ottoman Government and the Arabs, 1911 to 1918: a Preliminary Study of the Teşkilât-i Mahsusa*, Princeton, NJ: Princeton University Press, 1963.

85. Bilal Şimşir, *Malta Sürgünleri*, 5th ed., Ankara: Bilgi Yayınevi, 2009.

the

86. Baki Tezcan, "Ottoman Historical Writing," in José Rabasa [et. al.], *The Oxford History of Historical Writing: 1400-1800*, Oxford: Oxford University Press, 2012, pp. 192-211.

87. Elizabeth Thompson, *Justice Interrupted: The Struggle for Constitutional Government in the Middle East*, Cambridge, MA: Harvard University Press, 2013.

88. Khachig Tölölyan, "Elites and Institutions in the Armenian Transnation", *Diaspora*, Vol. 9, No. 1, 2000, pp. 107-136.

89. Khachig Tölölyan, "The Armenian Diaspora as a Transnational Actor and as a Potential Contributor to Conflict Resolution", Paper presented to the High Level Expert Forum entitled *Capacity Building for Peace and Development: Roles of Diaspora*, Toronto, Canada, October 19-20, 2006. Taken from URL: https://www.upeace.org/documents/news/2351_Booklet_ 1_UPEACE.pdf.

90. Esat Uras, *Tarihte Ermeniler ve Ermeni Meselesi*, 2nd ed., İstanbul: Belge Yayınları, 1987.

91. Uğur Ümit Üngör, *The Making of Modern Turkey: Nation and State in Eastern Anatolia*, 1913-1950, Oxford: Oxford University Press, 2011.

92. Ferhat Ünlü, "National Intelligence Organization", in Ümit Cizre (ed.), *Democratic Oversight and Reform of the Security Sector in Turkey*, Zurich and Munster: Lit Verlag, 2008.

93. Pierre Verluise, *Armenia in Crisis: The 1988 Earthquake*, Detroit, MI: Wayne State University Press, 1995.

94. Jay Winter, "Under the Cover of War: The Armenian Genocide in the Context of Total War, in Robert Gellately and Ben Kiernan (eds.), *The Specter of Genocide: Mass Murder in Historical Perspective*, Cambridge: Cambridge University Press, 2003.

95. Bat Ye'or, The Dhimmi: *Jews and Christians Under Islam*, Cranbury, NJ: Fairleigh Dickinson University Press, 1985.